Jewels

for

My Journey

by

Barbara Moon

Table of Contents

Dedication

I dedicate this book to JW, the kindest and wisest man I have ever known and without whom I would not be here. Also, I dedicate this book to the two Margarets in my life: the first, who was one of my sacrificial lambs to help me learn the things contained here, and the second, who is my best friend now.

Thanks

My deep thanks go first to Bob, my son who encouraged me and edited for me. Secondly, my thanks are to Greg and Chris who give me a home and the freedom to write. Thirdly, I thank Jodi, who stood by me through it all and to Jim, Jr., who has forgiven me for practicing my parenting skills on him. These are the wonderful children that help make my life worth living. Besides my children, I have one other friend whom I must thank. Debbie Sellmann has been a lifelong encouragement, only leaving me for a very short time. She truly loves me and tells me who I am.

PART ONE

MY FAITH JOURNEY

This is a story of my Spiritual journey of faith. I am an ordinary, everyday person who walks with an extraordinary God. A big part of my journey is about God healing my own wounds, as I walked with Him in ministry. I want to share my story so that others can have hope for rest and victory in their lives. I want to share so that those who long to know God in a deep, intimate way can see that it is possible. Because I am ordinary and not famous, outside my family of course, it is my deep desire that other ordinary people will benefit from reading how the Extraordinary God of the Universe worked in one ordinary person's journey of faith. And so I begin at the beginning.

I cannot remember a time in my life when I didn't know about God; nor can I remember a time when I did not love Him in one way or another. It would be difficult to credit all the people who have influenced my journey of faith, because I never knew the names of some of them. My journey began in the nursery where my parents took me to church as a very young child. I do remember the first Bible verse I memorized: "Be kind to one another." I was four years old.

I was born in Oak Ridge, Tennessee, towards the end of World War II. My daddy was one of the scientists who worked on the Manhattan Project. My mother stayed at home with us four children. Oak Ridge was a secret city, surrounded by mountains and fences. Guards allowed only the people who were supposed to be in the city to enter. Perhaps that was one reason my childhood was so happy. My parents allowed us to play all over the neighborhood. My favorite place was the creek behind our house. My sister Millie and I searched diligently for tadpoles and what we called "Indian clay." With this fabulous yellow clay we could make real bowls and other objects to dry in the sun. We walked, rode our bikes or even roller-skated to school. In the third or fourth grade any one who brought a note to school from home could walk to the nearby drugstore to eat lunch. They had the best hot dogs in the world. I learned to swim around the age of five at the city pool and have loved the water ever since.

FAITH AND SALVATION

In the summer of 1954, when I was nine years old, I attended Vacation Bible School at First Baptist Church. I couldn't wait to put on my shorts, shirt and sandals and ride to the church. It was so exhilarating to stand outside with all the children milling around waiting to enter the auditorium. I watched as the leaders began to line everyone up behind the privileged boys chosen to carry the waving American and Christian flags hanging from their long poles. And there between them was a girl—the one who had been chosen to carry the Bible. I longed to be picked some day to march in the front carrying a flag or the Bible. Although I knew the pledge to the American flag, I had not yet learned the pledges to the Bible and the Christian flag. I worked hard at memorizing them so that I could join in with the rest of the children as we recited.

It was during this week of VBS that I first understood that I needed to ask Jesus into my heart to be my personal Savior. One of the teachers talked to me and on June 20, 1954, I asked Jesus to be my Savior. Later in the week my parents took me talk to the pastor and I was baptized on July 4, 1954, wearing a white dress that my mother made for me. It would be years before I really understood all the theological aspects of my salvation, but for now I believed the verse that says salvation is through grace by faith and not of works, less any man boast. (Ephesians 2:8 and 9)

FAITH AND THE BIBLE

As I grew up, I continued to go to church every time the doors were open. I heard all the stories from the Bible in Sunday school. I learned about missions on Wednesday night and how to stand before my peers to present parts of the program on Sunday Nights. During elementary and early high school years, I had the privilege of participating in a program to help young people learn the Bible. It was a form of competition called a "Sword Drill." After memorizing many verses and where they were found, we competed to see who could find the verses the fastest. The rules were as strict as a sport and anyone who was skilled could move to higher levels of competition. Looking back, I am very thankful for that training. The verses I memorized are still with me and I've never had a problem finding a book of the Bible.

Someone back then loved teenagers enough to teach me that "All Scripture is inspired by God and profitable for teaching, for reproof, for correction, for training in righteousness, that the man of God may be adequate, equipped for every good work,"(II Timothy 3:16 and 17). They took the time to train some of us in the use of the Scriptures.

I specifically remember one person who had great influence in my life during my early teens. She taught the class for thirteen-year old girls. She cared for us, had us over to her house and taught us things, like "Don't date anyone you would not want to marry." That stuck with me throughout my dating years.

FAITH AND COMMITMENT

While growing up, it was common in my church to give altar calls that were for the purpose of becoming a Christian, joining the church or giving one's life to full time Christian service. Periodically there were calls to rededicate one's life to Christ. It seemed that one usually did this after some kind of sin or rebellion had taken place. Sometimes I went to the altar for rededication out of guilt that, as I later I knew, was really a longing to know God better. Because much of the teaching emphasized performing certain ways, I often felt that I was not good enough. My focus was on behavior and failure to measure up to whatever the current expectations were around me. But my heart was committed to God.

When I was eighteen, a few Sundays before I would be marrying Jim, my high school sweetheart, I answered a private altar call that came to me inside my heart. I sensed God asking me to make a distinct commitment to Christ to be the best Christian wife and mother I could be. I wasn't certain what that meant or how it would look, but it is what I wanted. The only place I knew to find out more about this calling was the church. So most of my life for the next several years centered around my family with Jim, going to church and church activities and enjoying friends from church. This didn't change if we moved. We just found another church to be involved in and made new friends. I longed to know God better, but was not certain how to go about it, so I continued being active in church, hoping that somehow I would find answers there. Life was generally good and busy with our two boys, Jimmy and Bobby. In 1968, we moved from Knoxville, Tennessee to a small town in Eastern Kentucky.

By 1969, we had our third son, Greg. I was very young and knew so little about real life. I loved being a wife and mother and church worker. I loved having friends to swap recipes and babysitting with. In our small community we had very few problems and my life just rocked along in daily living.

When Greg was about two months old, God shook my peaceful life. Greg was not thriving well. Since we had planned a trip back to visit our parents in Tennessee, I decided to take him to our previous pediatrician there. They ran some blood and urine tests, but could not find any thing. In my mother's heart, I still knew something was wrong, but I had no idea what it was. After we returned to Kentucky, Greg grew worse, now seldom keeping down formula, projectile vomiting across the room. I took him almost every day to the General Practitioners there in our small town. They prescribed medicine, but it did not help. For about three weeks Greg's whole digestive track was out of order, although through it all he continued to smile and coo and play as if nothing serious were wrong. I began growing desperate to find out what the problem was.

Finally a friend there in Kentucky said she would drive me an hour away to her pediatrician in the next town. This doctor took one look at Greg and said, "There is something wrong with his heart." At that moment, I saw my baby with the doctor's eyes and almost burst into tears. His color was bad, and he had lost weight. He went directly into the hospital there and after a few days of tests the doctor told us that there was definitely something wrong with his heart and we would have to take him to Lexington to the University of Kentucky Medical Center.

I vividly remember my faith journey during those few days. Since I loved to read, I had brought a book with me by Katherine Marshall, titled *Beyond Ourselves.* To this day, I don't remember many of the words from that book, but at the time God used it in my life. I said to Him: "This is your baby. He is Yours. You gave him to me. If You want to take him back, that is up to You. I just want what You want." I made this child-like statement of faith from deep within my heart knowing this was a situation I could not control.

After a few days at the first hospital to find a formula that would work for Greg, we drove to UK Medical Center. It was very late when we arrived. Up to this point I had not left the baby, and Jim and I were both exhausted.

We left Greg in the doctors' hands and went to the home of an acquaintance where we collapsed. The next morning we returned early to the Medical Center. During the night while we slept, the doctors had diagnosed our son with a terminal heart condition. The prognosis was "death within two years." I think Jim and I were both numb and all we could do was hold on to God. The next few weeks were rough and frightening as we adjusted to the news of Greg's condition.

The doctor that was in charge of our case told us that she had two very young patients still living with this condition. That was enough to keep us hoping, because all we heard was that she had two living. We did not hear that there were not any others. The doctors prescribed baby digitalis to help his heart beat and two weeks later Greg and I went home. Neighbors and family helped with the other two while Jim worked.

After being home about a week, Greg caught a cold. He and I had to go back to the first hospital (an hour from home) so that he could be under an oxygen tent. Jim and I quickly saw that this could become a regular issue every time he caught a cold. So we decided that we needed to move back to Tennessee where family and specialist doctors would be near by. For the next eight years we watched this child grow and thrive in spite of what we had been told. At that eighth yearly check-up Greg's cardiologist declared a miracle, saying he was well and his heart was normal. Today he is a grown man, married to Chris, with four girls of his own.

The next test of faith that came along was with our two older boys. They developed epilepsy. Now we had three children with somewhat major illnesses. We clung to God as best we knew how as we went on living out life. The older boys eventually outgrew their condition but during the interim, God used the crises to teach me a bit more about trusting Him. God was very important in my life and I looked to Him for help in times of need, but most of my faith journey then was very child-like and mostly based on church activities. I did not really know the totality of the Bible very well, though I knew stories and lots of verses. That was soon to change.

In 1972, our dream of having a little girl came true when Jodi was born. About a year later we moved to Huntsville, Alabama, where I made a new friend who really knew the Bible. She also knew Jesus better than she knew God and I knew God as Father better than I knew Jesus as Lord and Friend. As our friendship grew, each of us broadened the places that were lacking in the other. She grew to know God as Father and I came to know

Jesus as my intimate friend. We soon began a ladies' Bible study group. This was my first experience in a small group that was not a Sunday School class and I loved learning more and having the wonderful fellowship of other young mothers. By the end of that year, I understood that I needed to surrender my whole life to Jesus as Lord, so one day at home I prayed and told Him I wanted Him to have all of me, every area of my life and that He could do whatever He wanted with me. Soon I gave away my library of fiction books and began to study and read only my Bible, books about it, and books about the Christian life. The longing to know God deeply, that I had always sensed, grew deeper as I pursued that longing with all my heart. I wanted and begged Him to change things about me that were not like He wanted. Knowing Him became the focus of my life; yet the way I imagined and longed for that to be seemed just out of my reach.

FAITH GROWS

While in Huntsville God sent a couple across our path who worked with Campus Crusade for Christ. They were in the lay ministry section of CCC, which meant that they gave seminars on how to share one's faith with others and how to walk in the Spirit filled life. Their work was through churches rather than on college campuses. I had never met anyone like B. F. and Jane. B. F. shared how to know Christ with everyone he encountered. They were teaching their two teenagers the neatest things I'd ever heard.

As I got to know them and went to the seminars they taught, I grew another stretch, especially as I listened to them talk about walking with Jesus through the Holy Spirit. From them I learned that I could confess every sin I committed as soon as I did it and that it was forgiven and I could go on walking in the Spirit-filled life. The founder of CCC, Dr. Bill Bright, called this "breathing spiritually," just like we breathe physically. This was good news to a mother who often yelled at her children, something I hated doing. As I began to practice walking in the Spirit and depending on His power, changes came and I yelled less and less. B. F. and Jane taught me how to have a personal relationship with Jesus on a daily basis, how to pray and seek Him every day and take everything to Him. I asked Him often to change whatever about me that was not like Him.

Since loving and rearing my children was so important to me, I quickly applied the things I was learning to that area of my life. I made a "pact" with my oldest son, Jim, Jr., now eleven, to help me stop yelling at them in frustration. He agreed and we came up with a signal that he could do, or I could do if he were angry, to remind me that I was losing it. He would scratch the top of his head (or I would scratch mine to signal him) and when I saw it, I would back down and pray inside so that I would not exhibit the anger. It worked wonderfully and that became a precious memory for me. Jim, Jr. grew himself as he began to truly grasp the truth of walking with Jesus moment by moment. Perhaps God gave him a special place in his heart for middle school kids since he was so young when he learned this, because when he grew up he led the middle school youth program in a church for over ten years. That is a calling that few want to answer and it takes a very special person to walk it out.

B. F. and Jane introduced me to another group of speakers who traveled around the country speaking to churches that were part of the denomination that I belonged to. It was possible to hear them on cassette tapes and these men spoke passionately about walking moment by moment with Jesus. I bought and listened over and over to hundreds of tapes. One of the speakers, Peter Lord from Titusville, Florida, published a notebook on having a quiet time with God. I devoured it and used it every day for years. Ron Dunn from Dallas taught me how to increase my faith. He said it was by getting to know the object of one's faith. His ice story was part of what showed me a clearer way to know God better. It went something like this:

> I went to northern Michigan to do a conference. A friend wanted to drive me out to a nearby lake. As we drove along the lake, I noticed fishermen, sitting on the ice, out in the middle of the lake. They had cut holes in the ice and had dropped their lines into the water below. Since I am from the Southwest, I could not imagine sitting on ice to fish. Suddenly my friend turned toward the lake and told me he was going to drive out on it. I panicked. How could anyone drive a car out on to the lake? I was not about to go out on the lake in a car. I did not even want to walk out on the ice. When I nervously questioned my friend as to how all these people could do this, he quickly answered, "They know the ice."

Pastor Dunn's story helped me focus more on getting to know God for who He is. I read the Psalms over and over, five per day, which completes all of them in one month. In the Psalms I found God's character and could understand better who He is and what He is like. I read one Proverb per day for years, circling them each month, as there are thirty. In them I soaked in God's wisdom for living life His way. I spent hours in John 15 after I heard Pastor Dunn speak on that passage. Peter Lord spoke often, "Look at God's face, not His hand. See who He is, not what He does for you." Up until then I didn't even realize there was a difference. But when I made it personal as to how I wanted to be loved myself, it made sense. It certainly meant more to me to be loved for who I am than for what I do. As I grew in knowing God and His ways, I could see how the people fishing and driving on the ice trusted it to hold them, because they knew the ice; knew how thick it was and how strong. Like the ice fishermen, the more I knew God, the more I trusted Him. In the Scriptures, I soaked my heart and mind on who God is, what He is like, and how He works. My faith grew.

There were others during this time that contributed to my growing faith: Manley Beasley had a great testimony that he made into a Faith Workbook. Hudson Taylor, George Mueller and Reese Howells, men of the early twentieth century, told their stories through books I read. I was fascinated and longed to be like all of them. I was willing to go through anything to know God the way I was reading about. What did God want my next steps to be?

The next "natural" step for a good Christian, I had been taught, would be to go into "Full time Christian Service." A form of that occurred in 1976 when my husband and I joined the staff of Campus Crusade for Christ with the encouragement of B. F. and Jane. While on staff with CCC we had more teaching on sharing our faith with others, great teaching on marriage and family life, and training about leading small groups that would teach others how to do the things we were learning. Always the emphasis was on our relationship with Jesus and walking in the Spirit-filled life. We worked in groups that gave us great friends, fellowship and accountability.

But in spite of the great training and great fellowship we had with CCC, this was a very difficult time for me, for many reasons. Principally, it was a time of more striving and more feelings that I was not good enough. There were so many places I fell short, in everything. I would go to leaders for help, but most of them told me to perform better. My focus on performance grew. I continued to study and read and pray. But there were very big holes in my heart that I longed for God to fix. I wanted to trust Him more, to know Him deeper, to do His will.

One day on a personal retreat I was studying Philippians 3, again praying in my heart for God to be my all and make these verses real in my life. As I read down through the verses that I had read many times and memorized, especially verse 10, something new jumped out at me. I longed to "know Him and the power of His resurrection," but I had never noticed that the next phrase was "and the fellowship of His sufferings, being conformed to His death." Inside my heart I heard the Spirit ask me if I was willing for this part, too, as it was necessary. I did not have a clue what it would involve, but if suffering was part of it, I wanted it, and I answered Him, "Whatever You want." All I knew was that the longings in my deepest part were to know Him.

FAITH AND FINANCES

God took me at my word as He began to grow my faith during our years first with Campus Crusade and later with two other faith ministries, because we had to trust Him for our income. We were required to raise our own financial support in order to serve with these ministries. The burden of it rested on my husband, but it affected all of us as he gave up a good job to "live by faith," with a family of four growing children. At first it was very exciting as miracle after miracle took place. We prayed for new shoes for the kids and money appeared for them in different ways as I found money in our mailbox or cash in my purse after I had been to church. An old and dear friend in Tennessee gave us a car. Someone rear ended the car and totaled it, but it was still drivable. The insurance company gave us the choice of $900 or $800 and the car. We took the latter and painted "ROMANS 8:28" in big yellow letters across the back of the smashed trunk. A year later when we moved to Florida for training, we gave that car to friends who drove it another three years.

Before going to headquarters in California for our initial training with CCC, we sold our house and lived on the money. After our support base grew enough, Crusade moved our family to Orlando for training. At the end of that year our assignment was to Washington, D C where the cost of living was tremendously high. An acquaintance back in Huntsville heard our story of going into ministry and he came by to visit one night. He had been one of 19 survivors in a horrible airline crash the year before. Out of his settlement from the airline, he offered us $10,000 to buy a house in D. C. Over the next two years he paid for repairs to our dilapidated van. He loved us and became a close friend. On one long trip that we were required to make to Colorado, my sister and her husband in Texas paid for additional repairs to our old van. It was hard to put into words how all these miracles blessed us.

After the first year or so, the miracles slowly changed to tough lessons, forcing us to trust God when there were no visible miracles. Sometimes we trusted and sometimes we did not.

While in D. C. our oldest son needed braces. By faith we took him to an orthodontist. After the consultation, the dentist said he would do the braces for half price. That was great. But when that oldest also needed dermatology care, we waited too long to take him by faith and see what God would do. Scars were the price he paid for our unbelief that time. Living by faith was an up and down experience, but one I would not change for anything.

After living in Washington, D. C. for almost three years, our time with Campus Crusade came to an end. We moved to a suburb of Atlanta to serve with another Christian ministry. A lesson I was learning from the cassette tape speakers at that time was that "God has the supply before we have the need. If I don't get it, I didn't need it." Shortly after moving, three days went by without milk for four growing children. I was not a happy mother. But if I believed what I was hearing and was going to practice it, I had to say by faith, "Milk is not a need." It was not easy to say because I had always thought that milk was an every-day need.

In my struggle to believe God would provide food when it was not always visible, I did not always walk by faith. I cut corners by being very careful with food, even to the point of rationing. Slowly God taught me to look at Him and not the situations where finances were concerned. This took a very long time and I quite often fretted and complained. But deep in my heart I wanted to have to trust God like this so that I could know Him as Provider and it not just be words. Although it was very difficult, I believe it was good also for our children not to have everything they wanted or saw their friends having. They learned to pray for some of the special things they wanted, like Izod shirts and Guess jeans. One Christmas season after Greg said he wanted an Izod, we told him to ask Jesus for it. On Christmas day, he received three Izod shirts that we had not paid for. He saw that God even provided special things sometimes. When old enough, the children learned to work for money, doing part time jobs. They learned to be dependable and how to do a good job, how to work well. They learned to spend well (most of the time) and save.

There were many tough years as we lived by faith financially, but I grew and learned from it all, until finally, many years later, I could rest in knowing God's provision in a tangible, material area. Living by faith for our income is one of my favorite memories, with many miracles that we saw along the way. I most gratefully thank God for the privilege of learning Him that way.

FAITH – WHAT IS IT?

Before I continue with my journey of faith, I must answer the questions, "What is faith? Why does it matter? What makes it so important?" Hebrews, chapter eleven, verse one gives a good definition: "Faith is the substance of things hoped for, the evidence of things not seen." During my journey, even understanding definitions of faith was a growing process. I never had anyone to put it all together at once. Often we read this verse in Hebrews and think that faith is something that might be true or might happen if we hope enough. It is also common to think that the outcome is dependent on our other kinds of performance such as prayer or good behavior. We feel that we must pray enough or correctly enough. But these words say that faith is substance, something tangible. It is something we can count on. Something we can trust.

Hebrews 11:6a tells us "without faith it is impossible to please Him." Romans 14: 23b says that "whatever is not of faith is sin." The New Testament, in Romans, Galatians and Hebrews quotes Habakkuk 2:4. It says, "The righteous man shall live by faith." For me, these verses make it very important to know what faith is and to walk by and in it--if faith is what pleases God-- and we cannot please Him without it.

Then we read in Colossians 2:6, "As you therefore have received Christ Jesus the Lord, so walk in Him." Ephesians 2: 8 explains how we receive Jesus: "For by grace, through faith have you been saved, not of works, lest any man should boast." We received Christ by faith so the Colossians verse is again saying we walk in Him by faith.

Knowing what faith means has something to do with trusting and believing in things that cannot be touched, seen, handled, felt, or intellectually explained, while at the same time knowing somehow that they are real. We are so accustomed to living in the material, tangible world, that faith can seem crazy. I used to have a poster in my house that said, "Faith is walking to the edge of all the light you have—and taking one more step." This is a fairly good definition. The light would be a thing or circumstance we can see or touch or explain in the material realm. Taking one more step would put us into relying completely on the unseen and unexplainable. We cannot take that one more step without in some way knowing and depending on the *object* of our faith to be there in that first step into the unknown. That dependence only needs to be the size of a mustard seed (extremely small) in order to take that step.

When one takes that first step of faith and finds the object of faith (God) there and dependable in the small steps, then God will take those baby steps that we make and grow our dependence with greater steps of faith. Salvation, believing that Jesus will save me if I ask Him to, may be the first step of faith, but the rest of our lives, as we have seen from the verses above, we will take other first steps in different areas so that our walk with Him will be one of increasing faith. I saw that happen as I grew in knowing God and understanding more about myself. He has walked me through bigger and more difficult places to step out and believe Him, in spite of the material evidence. My definition of faith has settled to mean something like this: "Faith is saying and acting on whatever God says about something—and *whatever means whatever*." (Later I will learn that "Faith is a Person." Faith is Jesus Himself, and if I have Him, I have faith.)

FAITH AND DISCOURAGEMENT

While living in Washington, D. C., I had some problems that wore me down and ate away at my faith. Looking back at this time in my life, I can now see that God was beginning to show me more about the Philippians 3:10 verse about the fellowship of His suffering. The problems I had there are difficult to explain. I used to ask myself, "What was just my perspective and what was really true about the problems that arose?" Maybe it was some of both. But whatever the reasons were, my bent towards accepting myself based on performance and others' evaluations of me grew until I was almost non functional. It felt to me like the leaders around me were tearing down everything from my wardrobe to my personality. I now believe that part of the problem was too much legalism and not enough grace and unconditional love from the leadership, but I understood nothing of that during that time. I continued to read my Bible and pray, but there were days that I could hardly get off the couch, unable to believe anything I was reading from the Psalms. I would curl up on the couch and stay there until my husband came home or my children returned from school. This went on for several months before I understood any of what was going on in me.

While this pain went on and I searched and longed to understand it all, a couple from the Prison Ministry of CCC visited our home. They also had read books by and about the saints of old. We were fellowshipping at my kitchen table one night and they began sharing some ideas that were foreign to me. I was intrigued by their talk, though I did not really understand all that they were saying. "Well then you must know that Christians do not have the old nature anymore?" they asked. I hemmed and hawed since I had just told them that I had read all those books that they were talking about. Up to that statement, I had known what they were talking about. But this part of the conversation threw me. They continued to talk as if I did understand, giving me Scriptural bases for their words. I had no idea what they were talking about and I was too proud to tell them that I did not understand, though I heard enough to make me want to know more. As I listened, I knew I had to know for myself if what they were saying was true. Was it possible I might be at last hearing some answers for why I could not find God the way I wanted to? Was it possible I could understand what was going on? Finding out their words were true would turn out to be the *easy* part.

. After their visit I went straight to my Strong's concordance and looked up the two words they had explained: "old man" (old nature) and "flesh." There it was—they were two different words in the Greek. I had never been told this before, nor had I noticed it in my studies. I began going over every passage that contained these two words. Soon I was convinced that this couple had told me the truth. I now believed, "Christians do not have the old nature." But I did NOT know why that was important or why it made any difference. I had no idea how to bring my pain and this new knowledge together. The next months continued a downward spiral of failure. Where could I get help? I knew two or three other people that were familiar with this teaching, but they were far away in Georgia.

As the situation in D. C. worsened, my husband and I were hurting so badly that we turned to a few friends for help. A dear pastor from Maryland and a Family Life leader from CCC helped us keep our heads above water. B. F., the man we had met in Huntsville, encouraged us to call his new boss, head of another ministry. Soon we were packing to move again, this time hopefully the last for our young teenagers that had moved so often already.

We were going to Atlanta and hope bubbled inside me that the friends there would be able to explain what was going on with me.

By now I was a devastated failure at living the Christian life. I had studied and read my eyes out. I was getting to know God in a deeper way and loving Him with all my heart, but rest and victory continued eluding me. Hebrews 4: 9 and 10 promised rest: "There remains therefore a Sabbath rest for the people of God. For the one who has entered His rest has himself also rested from his works; as God did from His." Jesus said, "Come unto Me you who are weary and heavy-laden and I will give you rest. Take My yoke upon you, and learn from Me, for I am gentle and humble in heart: and you shall find rest for your souls. For My yoke is easy and My load is light." (Matthew 11:28-30) In my heart I knew these verses were true, but they were not real in my experience. All I studied and read said the rest of faith was possible. I struggled on, looking for some kind of key to make it work, feeling more and more like a failure who was no good and could not do anything right.

FAITH AND THE EXCHANGED LIFE

When we finally arrived in the Atlanta area in early 1980, I clung to the friends there that were a few steps ahead of me in learning that Christians do not have the old nature any more. I just about drove them crazy with my questions and my discouragement. They told me I could not understand spiritual truth through my intellect, but that I had to allow God to reveal it to me. I did everything I could think of to make that happen. I struggled and struggled. I begged. I gave up. I listened. I tried some more. The couple from the Prison Ministry had given me a set of tapes with messages by Bill Gillham and his wife Anabel. Although I had listened to the tapes while still in D. C., they were like a foreign language to me. I persevered though, because I knew I was hearing something life changing. Finally after about the 50th hearing, God used those tapes to help me see what I was struggling so much to understand. That day when I finally understood, the "revelation" almost knocked me to my feet. I heard the Holy Spirit tell me that I was not a terrible, rotten no good bum (which is what I called myself inside every time I failed to perform), but that I was holy, righteous and blameless and a new person in Christ.

Finally, in spite of my efforts and striving, God revealed to me that my life of striving to be loved and accepted was not necessary and why knowing about the old nature made a difference. Pieces began to fall together. The passages, books and tapes I was devouring began to make sense and I had some answers to my questions. The truths were not new, except to us, but I felt like I was in a revival movement that had just begun here in our little group of people in Atlanta. Now there are many modern books about the "Exchanged Life," "knowing who we are in Christ," and/or "grace and freedom," but in the early '80's God shined a new spotlight on the old truths. Though these truths were there in the Scripture and in the old writings, I never heard any explanations about them until I met that couple from Campus Crusade Prison Ministry and listened to the Gillhams.

After moving to Atlanta, I gave copies of the Gillham's tapes to Duane and Tom, the friends who had been helping us, and they had in turn passed them on to a family member of Dr. Charles Stanley, pastor of First Baptist Atlanta. Through Dr. Stanley, Dr. Bill Gillham and his wife, Anabel eventually came to Atlanta in person. What a privilege to hear and see them. I nearly had their talks memorized from listening to the tapes. Dr. Gillham put the truths into catchy stories and memorable pictures that were easy to follow. More and more people's lives were being healed of negatives from their pasts as we all understood the good news that we did not have to work or strive to be accepted and loved by God, because His love was not based on our performance. There was great freedom and rest in understanding *all* that happened to us when receiving Christ as Savior and Lord. (Presently Bill and Anabel's books and messages can be bought on their website—www.lifetime.org.)

Here in Atlanta, along with the Gillham's, Dr. Charles Solomon of Denver, Colorado, was as a very key person to spotlight the beginning of the current movement about freedom in Christ. Dr. Solomon's testimony, books and counseling model helped many of us as he also put the ideas into easy to understand illustrations and diagrams. Duane and Tom were already using Dr. Solomon's model in an experimental counseling office under the CCC umbrella. After the trial year, Tom and Duane decided to open their own office under Dr. Solomon's umbrella. Hurting people poured in for help, wanting to hear the good news of grace and freedom. We often met together for fellowship and in a very short time our numbers grew from 6 to over 100. Other counselors wanted to get training for this model of counseling and soon other counseling ministry offices sprouted up all over Atlanta. We outgrew the facility where we were meeting together, as more people understood the "new" truth and soon these large meetings faded away.

Newly trained counselors settled in to help hurting people in various parts of the city and Jim and I began our own small group in our part of the city.

Jim and I loved living in Atlanta and being part of this movement. Jim felt as though he had found his niche as we attended Dr. Solomon's seminars and workshops to hear his model first hand. His niche was counseling and we soon began our own "Exchanged Life Ministries" with small group follow-up for the counselees. We met together in our home or homes of friends. I continued to listen to Dr. Gillham and continued to read and study the Scriptures, now digesting without striving.

We felt privileged to hear Dr. Solomon in person. His explanations and diagrams helped me to see that I am a three-part person—spirit, soul, and body (1 Thessalonians 5:23). When I accepted Christ, He came literally to live in my spirit. (Ezekiel 36:26) In *that place* there is nothing wrong with me and I am totally accepted (Ephesians 1: 6b), loved (Romans 5:5, 8), righteous (Romans 10:4, 10), holy and blameless (Ephesians 1:4). It was easy to see the parallel with the Old Testament Tabernacle, which was made up of three parts. My human spirit is like The Holy of Holies where no sin can abide. It is where the Holy Spirit lives. My soul, or personality is like the Holy Place, and my body is like the Outer Court. The most important passages that I came to understand are in Romans and Ephesians.

The diagrams that Dr. Solomon taught about Romans 6 helped me to see my past in a different light. I needed different light on my past, as I had suffered a serious trauma when I was a young teenager. I will talk about this in detail in the Jewels from JW. Dr. Solomon's explanations (and those of the others who were now teaching and writing of these things) of what it means to be "In Christ," changed almost everything I believed about growing and walking with Jesus. The book of Ephesians uses a variation of the phrase "in Him" about ten times just in the first chapter. There is a passage in Hebrews 6:20-7:10 (from Genesis 14 18:20) that talks about Melchizedek, a priest who met Abraham and to whom Abraham paid a tithe. Hebrews says that Levi paid the tithe as well, though he was not born yet. Levi was "in Abraham," in his loins, as verse 10 says. Other passages became clearer as I read my Bible with new eyes of understanding. I was finding who we are in Christ everywhere and wanted to share with everyone I knew.

As the understanding of what it meant to be in Christ settled in to my heart, Dr. Solomon's explanations of Romans 6: 1-14 and Ephesians 1:6 were especially eye opening. Understanding that I was now in Christ, made it easy to see that being in Christ means that whatever happened to Him happened to me (my old self was crucified with Him, I was buried with Him and raised up and seated in the Heavenliest with Him) Since the very life I had received when receiving Christ was His life, the whatever is true of Him is true of me (in my personhood, in my spirit). (1 John 5: 11-13) Christ's life is Eternal life, which is life that has no beginning and no ending. When I was taken out of Adam's life and placed into Christ's life at salvation, I received a new life, the very eternal life of God that is without beginning or end, not affected by time. Jesus said that He is the "I AM." As I saw myself in Christ, in His Eternal life, some old childhood wounds began to heal (more on that later). By faith, I had a "new childhood" and a new past when I was put into Christ. I already knew somewhat that He came to live in me (somewhere in my heart, whatever that was), but I had never heard that I was "In Him."

For more information and diagrams, see Dr. Solomon's book, *Handbook to Happiness*, p.40. On the next page is my rendition of his line diagram. He uses a slanted vertical line to illustrate being "In Adam" before salvation, a family line that is headed for separation from God, or hell. The other line, drawn horizontally, represents Christ's Eternal Life. At salvation, according to Romans 6 and other passages, we die to the Adam life and are reborn into Christ's life. Although I had trusted Jesus for my salvation, I did not really know how to trust Him for my growth. Finally, I was hearing how to trust Him with the growth and changes I wanted to see happen.

FAITH AND THE BIBLE—AGAIN

As I began re reading my Bible, it was like I had never read the New Testament before. I began noticing verb tenses, how many of them were past tense. For example these verses from Ephesians: (Italics mine) "He *has blessed* us with every spiritual blessing," " . . .you *were sealed* in Him with the Holy Spirit of promise," "you *were dead* in your trespasses and sin, in which you *formerly walked*," ". . . *made* us alive together with Christ . . .. *raised* us up with Him and *seated* us in the Heavenly places in Christ Jesus." Then from Colossians: "in Him you *have been made* complete," "you *were* also circumcised with a circumcision made without hands," "having *canceled* out the certificate of debt . . .He *has taken* it out of the way," "Since you *have died* with Christ," "for you *have died* and your life is hidden with Christ

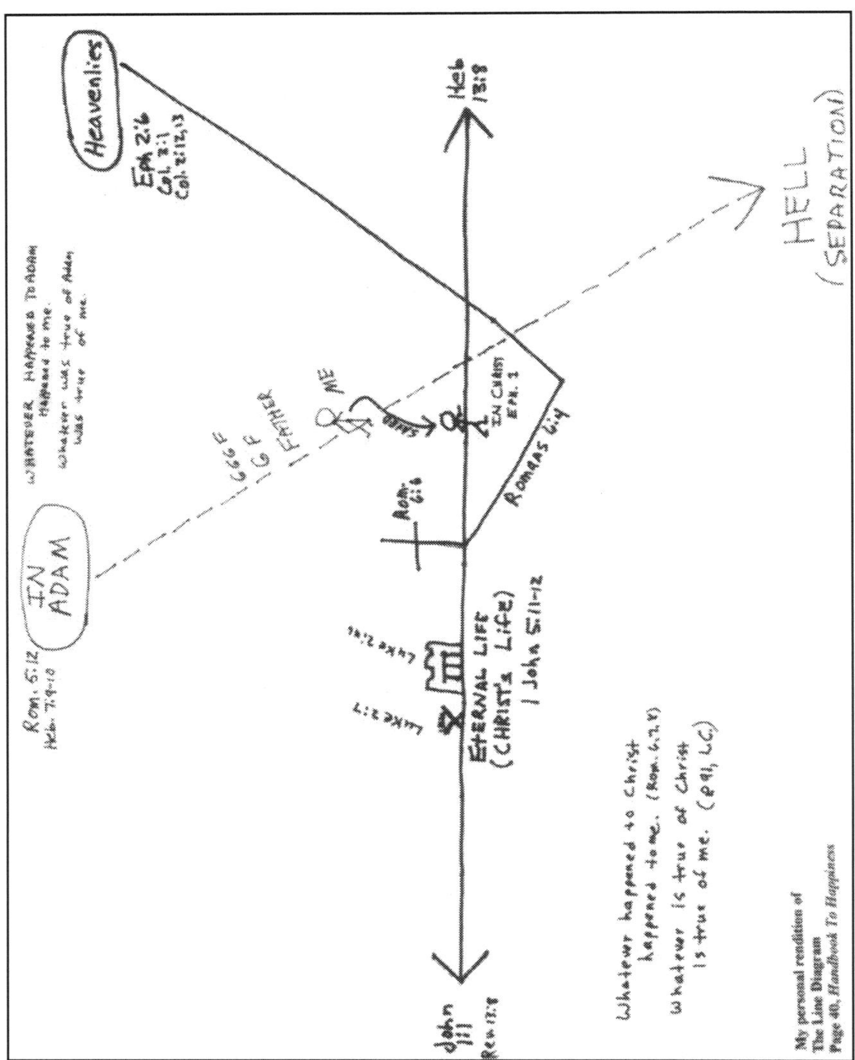

Figure 1. *My personal rendition of "The Line Diagram" from Charles Solomon's* Handbook to Happiness.

in God." These are just a few of the many verses that say what is *already* true of us.

Finally light dawned on my struggle. I knew that faith was a key, not striving and trying. I had practiced walking by faith in some areas, but not about my identity. I was learning that I was to walk in my identity the same way I received Christ—by faith. So by faith, because it did not feel or look so, I began to say over and over to myself, "I am holy, righteous, blameless, accepted, loved, and I really don't want to sin." This changed my thinking so drastically, that I felt like a new person. One day on a retreat, while I was reading the book *Birthright* by David Needham, God showed me more deeply that I truly am a new creation. When I received Christ, something new was created, not just added. I had been taught that Jesus was added to my life while the bad me remained there. Coupled with the other things I was learning, Dr. Needham's statements cleared my mind completely to understand I Corinthians 5:17 and Ezekiel 36:26, that God had made something new that never was before, a new me, a new creation. THIS was why it made a difference to know there was no old nature anymore! What I believed about myself and Christ determined how I lived—whether I lived by striving (thinking I have to perform) or resting (knowing I am accepted in the Beloved not based on performance.)

I wanted to share all I was learning with everyone I knew, like I had found the answer to cancer. It was like being born again all over. Getting to know God took on a whole new meaning. I did not need to fear anything from Him or worry about my sinfulness. I was loved and accepted in the Beloved and sin was no longer my focus.

FAITH AND SIN

When sharing what I was learning with someone new, they always brought up the BIG QUESTION: "But what about sin? You are saying you are perfect, holy and righteous. You can't be saying we don't sin anymore. This is heresy." I had several things to say about these questions.

These questions arise when there is talk about a new life in Christ based on grace and freedom because we have been taught to be "sin conscious." My old cassette friend, Peter Lord taught about this as well in the early 80's.

He told the story of a baby eagle that fell from its nest onto the forest floor, into a nest of baby turkeys. It went something like this:

> This baby eagle grew up with the turkeys, eating their food, following their mother turkey, walking around in the forest, and doing turkey things. Sometimes the baby eagle felt an inner sense that he was not made for the forest floor. His wings drug the ground as he walked, where his brothers' wings were short and stubby. But, after all, he was a turkey, so he did what the turkeys did. One day someone came and told him that he was not a turkey at all, that he was an eagle. Eagles could soar above the forest, through the air, in the clouds. The little eagle wanted to argue, but the other bird convinced him to at least check it out. He led the eagle to the edge of a very high cliff. "Jump!" he cried to the eagle. "You can fly! Trust me, you can fly! You are not a turkey. You are an eagle!" The eagle was very frightened as he looked down at the canyon below, but something stirred in his heart. He jumped. He spread his great wings and the wind caught him and lifted him high above the cliff. He soared and floated. He dove and soared some more. He was an eagle. "I am an eagle!" he shouted as his helper joined him in flight. "I don't ever want to scrounge on the forest floor again."
> Paraphrased from *Turkeys and Eagles*, by Peter Lord, 1997

In addition to this story, Peter Lord was telling everyone who would listen that we no longer had to be sin conscious. We needed to be "righteousness conscious." John 16:8 says, "When He (the Holy Spirit) comes He will convict you of sin, righteousness, and judgment." Pastor Lord would ask audiences if anyone had ever been convicted of righteousness. Few raised their hands. If he asked an audience to write down how many times they had sinned today, they would write large numbers without even thinking about it. He helped many of us to see that we really did not sin all that much. And when we did, we could confess it and go on. This was one of the places my new definition of faith helped me. "Say whatever God says about something—and whatever means whatever." Confess (say the same thing God says) and God will forgive. (I John 1:9) If I believe He forgives, I say what He says, "I am forgiven." I may not feel like it, look like it or act like it, but I stand on what He says.

Standing on what God says was becoming real to me in many areas. To say things like, "I am holy, righteous, blameless, loved, accepted, or whatever," might look like I am crazy. But it is very important to understand what and where we are perfect, holy, righteous and blameless. I was learning to separate who I am from what I do. Of course, all that we *do* is not perfect. All through our culture, we are hammered with the idea, "You are what you do." If you act badly, you are bad. If you lie, you are a liar. This is not the way God sees things. He does not see us through what we do. To make us laugh and see the untruth of "you are what you do," Dr. Solomon used to say, "So if you moo are you a cow?" Mooing does not make me a cow, nor does barking make me a dog. Being born in a Christian home does not make me a Christian. Being born in a garage does not make me a car. Though these are obvious examples, believing I am what I do is a very difficult concept to unlearn!

The most difficult place to unlearn this concept is when it concerns sinning. Committing a sin does not make a Christian a sinner. (Paul addressed his letters to the "saints," even to the sinning Corinthians.) We will often accept that good works do not make a person a Christian, but we find it harder to accept that sinning does not make a Christian a sinner. Jesus died to change who we are, to crucify the old nature, not just to forgive us for our sins. (More on that later) Before receiving Christ, we were sinners who did good things once and a while. Now Christians are saints who sin once and a while

.

Understanding who we are in Christ does not diminish the seriousness of sin as some fear. It simply takes our eyes off of believing we are loved and accepted by what we <u>do</u> instead of by who we <u>are</u>. Sin is serious and should be spoken to, dealt with and ended. But sin consciousness as a <u>focus</u> can take our eyes off of the loving, accepting, forgiving Savior who is our very life.

The book of Galatians helped me understand this concept of how we're accepted as well. Whenever I read it, I substitute the word "behavior" or the word "performance" for the word "Law." This makes it clearer to me what we are free from. I was living as if under the Law my whole Christian life, until this period of time. And sadly, when I was under the Law, I put others under it as well, loving them and accepting them based on their behavior or performance. This kind of law-based living does not make Jesus' version of the first two commandments work very well. "Love your God with all your heart, soul and mind and your neighbor as yourself." Unfortunately, we often do love our neighbor the same way we love ourselves and that is not always with God's kind of love—when it is based on performance. *Agape* love has no place in it for conditions.

FAITH AND PRAYER

Another big change that came in my walk with the Lord was in the way I pray. I had my notebook, my Bible, my lists and my personal desires. Nearly every day I went to God with my needs and wants. There were prayers for my children, my husband, my country, my church, everyone. But my deepest longings were for God to change me. I begged and pleaded with Him all the time. On the top of my personal list was "Please, Lord, give me a gentle and quiet spirit." (I Peter 3:4) My personality type is not one of the more popular personalities. Nor are my Spiritual Gifts—prophecy and discernment. I let that unpopularity influence how I looked at myself. I did not like myself very much. Some of the things others rejected about me, I rejected as well. For certain, some things needed to be changed, but many needed to be accepted. I did not always distinguish the two very well.

One day in my time with God, as I was going over my lists again, I asked Him once more for that gentle and quiet spirit. I heard quietly in my heart, "You already have one. Now thank me for it." Ohhh, Nooo! How could that be? How could I do that? Not a chance! My feelings screamed. But my spirit knew—Yes! That would be faith. Not only would it be faith (agreeing with God no matter what), but since it was His voice I was hearing, it would also be obedience. So I said and wrote, "Thank you, Lord, that I have a gentle and quiet spirit." It was one of the most uncomfortable things I ever did. It went against all my feelings and self- evaluations.

Did anyone else notice right away that I already had a gentle and quiet spirit? I don't think so. Not for a very long time. But I had to say it was so from then on, faithing what God says, NOT going by how I felt, looked, sounded, or acted. This was faith. This was pleasing to God. This was another big step in my new life and new walk.

As I read my Bible with new eyes, I noted in Galatians 5:22-23, that the fruit of the Spirit was a singular word—fruit. Furthermore, I began to understand that the fruit is a person—Jesus Himself. As this understanding grew deeper, I could never again ask Jesus for patience. If I have Him, I have patience. So my prayers changed to "Thank you, Lord, I have Your patience, You Yourself are my patience. Thank you that you are patience in me in this situation." My view of faith broadened as I saw that He Himself is faith and the One faithing through me. I quit asking for qualities and began thanking

Him that I already had them, especially when it was clear in the Scriptures what He wants for us or what He is like.

God deepened my self-acceptance again a few years later as I was praying, writing in my journal, as is my way, when He clearly told me to sign my name as "Bringer of Joy." That was outrageous. No way! I was not going to say I was a Bringer of Joy. But again, that quiet prompting reminded me about faith. It is saying what God says—no matter what. So I signed my name from then on as Bringer of Joy, or BOJ. Today, many years later, I most of the time even look and act like that. God's changes are often very slow, but they are sure. My desires for growing and changing began to come true when I understood walking by faith, saying what He says and not going by my feelings or actions.

FAITH AND UNION

In the mid 1980's I met some other people who carried me a bit further in my journey of faith and freedom. They built upon the foundation from Drs. Solomon and Gillham. Norman Grubb was in his nineties when I met him. His words were somewhat stronger than those I had heard earlier, and I began to read his books and listen to him as he taught. Norman's words closed some kind of small gap in my thinking. Over and over he talked of our union, our oneness with Christ. He said there is no separation between Christ and us, in our spirit where He lives in us, as us. He did not say we cannot sin, but rather helped me focus less on sin and even deeper on who I am. His words "no separation," are where I live to this day. They changed the way I think, the way I talk, the way I pray, the way I live. More pieces fell together. I no longer yearn or beg to get closer to God. One cannot get any closer than "one" with a person. (1 Corinthians 6:17) By faith I know I am one with Him and I watch for intrusive thoughts or beliefs that may hint at separation. I feel sad when I hear words to music begging to get closer to God. I feel sad when I hear people begging God for things they already have. I hear it everywhere—the longings I used to have, when I didn't know that I am one with Christ and He is Everything, my very life. (Colossians 3:4)

Norman Grubb had another phrase that stuck with me. He always talked about "What you take, takes you." This was his definition of faith. I have found it to be very true. He illustrated this idea using the examples of eating something or learning a new job skill. If I eat an apple, the apple becomes me. If I take "cooking," I become a cook. If I take carpentry, I become a carpenter. First I have to study or "take" cooking or carpentry, but later I can say, "I am a _________(cook or a carpenter)" when it has taken me over.

This became real to me when I was learning to drive a school bus in the early 1980's. It was a new experience though I had driven cars for years. There were many things to remember. In order to park, I had to set the gear to park, turn off the key, set the air brake, and remove the key. I memorized this by rote. Driving became easier as I practiced. As the days went by, I began to notice that I was parking "automatically." I no longer had to take it-- it had taken me. I was a bus driver. (Of course there was more to it than parking.)

Using Norman's words, I could apply this new learning experience in the physical world to my spiritual walk of faith. Whatever I take, will take me. If I "take" that I am a gentle and quiet spirit, that will "take" me and someday it will show in my walk. I could take that I really do not want to sin, and that would become real in my experience. This taking by faith would also include things I did NOT want to take me, such as lies from Satan.

Satan likes to program us with false thinking about ourselves to keep us defeated. For example, some of my "tapes" said things like, "I can't do anything right." "I have to try harder." "I can do that by myself." "I hate myself." "All authorities are always right." "I'm just a rotten, no good bum." So it became important to notice what I was "taking" to be sure that I was taking only truth that God says about me and not taking any lies based on my behavior or my past actions.

Two other people that had been mentored by Norman Grubb were very important to my journey of faith. Laurie Hills and Dan Stone visited our home many times and taught us other ways of knowing our union with Jesus. My favorite lessons from Dan are his line illustration from II Corinthians 4:18, his swing illustration about feelings, his explanation about the two sides of the cross, and his description of Union from Genesis 3. Second Corinthians 4:18 says, "while we look not at the things which are seen, but at the things that are unseen; for the things that are seen are temporal but the things that are not seen are eternal." Dan spoke on that verse constantly, reminding us that God's stuff is more real than what we can see and touch and smell and hear.

This comes in very handy when circumstances are not looking very good. He says that we can use a line to help understand this verse. We can draw the imaginary line anywhere-- in the air, on the dash of the car, or in our minds. We then remember what is temporal and what is eternal, what is reality and what is lies, what is fact and what is appearance. All things above the line are eternal. This is where true reality resides. Below the line are temporal, temporary and passing away things. The seen things are below the line, the unseen above the line.

After drawing our line, we can apply this to a circumstance that looks negative. What does God say? What is eternal? Where is faith? Above the line. This curtails worry and fretting. God is bigger than what we can see and touch. It lets us see that He is in everything and that there are no accidents and we can rest and trust in Him right in the middle of the circumstance.

Dan has gone to be with the Lord, but he left a book behind called, *The Rest of the Gospel, When the Partial Gospel Has Worn You Out*, published in 2000 by One Press.

FAITH AND FEELINGS

Dan uses an ordinary childhood swing to explain about feelings. Like the swing, our feelings are *meant* to swing. It is no easier to change or fix feelings than it is to tack or nail a swing to only go in one direction. Feelings are just feelings. Sometimes they are helpful and trustworthy and sometimes they are deceitful as they pertain to past events. They do not define who we are as we look to God alone for truth. But neither do we try to tack our feelings over on the "good feeling" side of that swing. "Bad feelings" are part of life, too. We just don't go by that swing's natural motion. Chapter 6 of Dan's book explains this in detail.

One thing about feelings that I would like to clarify here is that sometimes we use the phrase, "going by your gut." This has the connotation of going on how I feel. For me, "going by my gut" is equivalent to following my heart, which would be following my spirit in union with God's Spirit. It is a sense of knowing something deep down and emotions (feelings) may or may not line up with this knowing.

FAITH AND APPEARANCES

Laurie Hills, the other person who taught me union, helps clarify the struggle about feeling and knowing. I have asked her to insert her own writing here so that it can be very clear. She uses the passage of Hebrews 4:12 to clarify her "Heart Illustration."

THE ENVIRONMENT OF THE SOUL by Laurie Hills

Hebrews 4:12 is the Centerpiece for my writing, but there are some things to be said before I begin digging for the treasure found there.

The book of Hebrews was most likely written by Paul, or by someone whom he mentored. Jesus and his disciples were gone from the scene, so he is writing to second or third generation Christians, whose excitement about having known someone who knew Jesus or knowing someone who knew one of His disciples was waning.

The veil had been rent in the Temple concurrent with Jesus' Crucifixion, indicating that the ultimate sacrifice had been made in His Son. There was no longer place for animal sacrifice. The Temple organization, however, still continued and Legalizers, those who hung onto the Law, were working hard on these discouraged Christians, hoping to get them back "in the fold." It must have been a strong temptation to have something tangible, like the temple worship and laws, even knowing that they were circumcised, by which they could operate. In Hebrews 12:12 the writer talks about "strengthening their feeble arms and weak knees".

The writer began his book with a chapter that presented Jesus Christ as God. The second chapter made it clear that Jesus Christ was representative man. After that needed review, strongly reminding them of The God-Man in their midst, the writer proceeds to chapter three. His purpose here is to remind them of their ancestors' sorry plight. God had

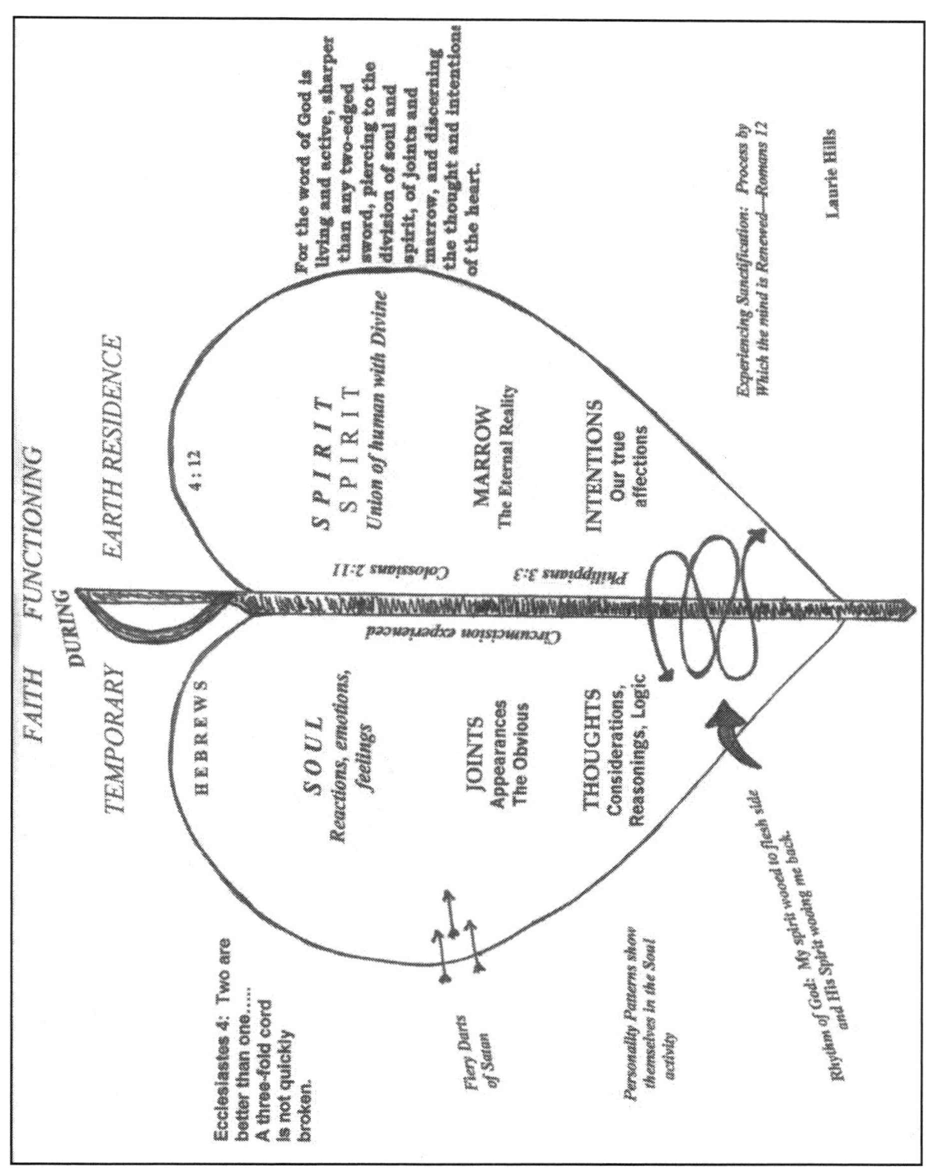

Figure 2. *An illustration of Laurie Hill's "Heart" diagram.*

delivered them from Egypt and slavery and led them through the desert, yet faith had not developed in them and of them He said, "They shall never enter MY REST". He uses the word TODAY in chapters 3 and 4, speaking of times when He had yearned for His nation to learn faith so they would enter His Rest.

The writer to the Hebrews was eager, with God's own yearning, for them to enter into His rest. God's rest is literally His Life. Our temptation as Christians is to "live our own lives" and then ask God to fix the resulting brokenness. This verse is a picture of "the way life works in Jesus" as opposed to life not working. You may have heard this verse, as had I, many times. My "reading through" it, as I did most of the Bible until I was 40, saw nothing more than words here. Then one day there was an "AHA!" or an "OH, I SEE!!!"

The verse: "FOR THE WORD OF GOD IS QUICK AND POWERFUL AND SHARPER THAN ANY TWO-EDGED SWORD, PIERCING EVEN TO THE DIVIDING ASUNDER OF SOUL AND SPIRIT AND JOINTS AND MARROW AND IS A DISCERNER OF THE THOUGHTS AND INTENTIONS OF THE HEART." Hebrews 4:12. Dear Lord, I ask for Your Spirit to produce in the readers Your own AHA!!. Thank You for what You are doing.

Please keep referring to the Heart picture as you read, especially if you work best when words are accompanied by a picture.

THE WORD OF GOD

The Word, the Bible, is the source from which all eternal truth comes. We may or may not, as Christians, have found the joy there is in reading and studying the Word. Perhaps our association with it has been through Sunday School, church, Bible Studies, Christian radio, parents or a friend. We, as Christians, having had it placed in our computer brains and in our feeling hearts by the Spirit of God are blessed beyond measure. Why? Because when we are irritated, frustrated, underrated, attacked, hurt, ill, the Faithful Spirit acts. He sends the Word of God plunging down between our soulish ways and the Presence of the Spirit living in us to remind us of our True Identity in Jesus Christ. With the Word established in our minds, we are shown the contrast between our soul storm and His Presence in our spirit, waiting to do what He does. As we take our stand in faith, He takes the storm and replaces it with His Peace, Wisdom, Patience – whatever the situation requires.

SOUL AND SPIRIT

The first discernment the Spirit gave to me was simply that there is a difference between Soul and Spirit. I had assumed that Soul was the word that described all our inner activity. This verse and another of Paul's verses (1st Thessalonians 5:23) clearly delineate between soul and Spirit. So where does Spirit come in? Here is a verse, amazing to me when it was pointed out. " He that is joined to the Lord is one spirit with Him." (1st Cor. 6:17) Do you see that on the right side of the heart is Spirit: His Spirit and ours having become one? I had thought, "I am a Christian. I pray to God outside me. I can get my sins forgiven when I ask. I will go to heaven when I die, but for now, for the most part I am separated from Him. I must just be as good as I can be so I will for sure go to Heaven." NOOOO!! When He wooed me into recognizing Him as this sinner's Savior, so much more happened than I knew anything about. When He came in, the old spirit of self for self (satan) went out and His Spirit became one with my spirit. Then no longer a lost sinner; I was a new creature; a redeemed saint. Do you believe that about you? He is right there, joined to your spirit, one with you. Ask Him to be your Truth about it and keep on saying that it is true because His Word says so. It is TRUE. As you give assent to that being TRUE in you, it will finally take over in your soul. Satan whispers, "Yeah, you're saved, but you're still the old you." (The Deceiver makes us think that we are saying that LIE.) NOOOOOOOOOOO!! God sees us as that new person in Him. He is at work on the patterns in our soul that were formed during the years we weren't His. He is changing the environment of our soul.

SOUL

That began to unravel my knotty problem about being a good enough Christian. As I looked at the strange list in the verse and saw that the sword of the Spirit – the Word of God, divided them from each other. (See Heart) I actually saw the occupants of soul and the occupants of spirit. Soul stands for that which is not spirit as in this illustration: EMOTIONS, REACTIONS, APPEARANCES AND THOUGHTS within the Soul. They can be here today and gone tomorrow, or in the next minute. They are as undependable as is the shape of a cloud on a windy day. Often they are wonderful unless we choose to live out of them --depending on them for our life. My feelings about me having to be good, but finding I couldn't be good enough were all I thought I had, so my experience as a Christian, although convincing myself that I looked OK on the outside, was guilt and self-condemnation on the inside – most of the time. Once in awhile, there would be a good day and I would think I was a really good Christian. It was a bumpy existence without rest. I was living a soul-based existence – my experience lived out of my feelings, thoughts, reactions.

Satan lost a lot of influence over my soul when some kind person told me that temptation was not sin. It is only sin if I pursue it and do it. Now there was a giant "AHA".

JOINTS

Someone bent their arm and pointed to their elbow, asking if this was really their elbow. I said that of course it was, but they asked me to look across the sword (on the Heart) to the word there: marrow. They already knew what I was just then learning: that the elbow couldn't survive without the marrow inside that is its life. That part was easily understood, but what did it have to do with this verse? There was another AHA for me. The elbow stood for Appearances or the obvious, while the marrow represented the Eternal Real: Jesus Christ. We can't see Him. As we choose trusting HIM, we experience Him.

All of a sudden I became aware of the importance to me of appearances. In the beginning it was my dissatisfaction with my clothes and hair and my long, narrow, flat feet, rather than my delight in the MARROW – God Himself -- dwelling and working in me. Those appearances began to seem like very small potatoes to me when my daughter rebelled and the Spirit asked me to "see through" that heart breaking situation rather than "seeing at" it. I began taking a stand against believing in the appearances, such as, " I have been a very bad mother and perhaps I have lost her". Those appearances seemed real in the flesh and Satan, the detractor, was attempting to keep me believing that things would never be different. The Spirit was faithful to remind me of God's Presence and pick me up when I became overwhelmed by what appeared the only reality of the sad situation. The Spirit of Truth required one thing only of me: that each time I was tempted to "believe in the appearances" I would return to the TRUTH. Finally the tempter lost his power in this battle and I was settled in the fact that the Lord had my daughter and was at work to bring about His Best. Among the blessings God brought forth is the fact that He healed both daughter and mother. I should say that it took time. One of the things I learned along the way was to simply give her to God. It was like breathing fresh mountain air to see her by Faith in Him.

When my husband began showing signs of Alzheimer's disease, I thought it couldn't be happening to us, but the Faithful Spirit reminded me that "seeing at" would only reap havoc in my soul and bring no glory to God. Actually, God got much glory out of those years and I remember them as a blessing. The joints (appearances) we see and feel first. That is good, since our negative reaction is exactly what opens our helpless souls to the Marrow (God right there in the middle of the mess working His great good.) Romans 8:28 fits and it must, since the message of the Gospel in action is in this Hebrews 4:12 verse, sort of hidden away, waiting for those who have become hungry enough to find it.

SPIRIT

When we accept Him and He comes in, we don't know it, maybe for a long time, but He is there within accomplishing the purposes necessary for the Life of Jesus to take over our Soul. When I was first seeing the wonder of this verse and saw that Intentions were listed on the Spirit side. I couldn't see how my Intentions could be found on the Spirit side, since doubts dogged my steps about goodness. The Spirit reminded me that ever since I had accepted Him at the age of nine the INTENTION of my heart was to please Him. My thoughts and feelings had taken me on many rides not designed to please Him. One day another "Oh, I see" happened. When the Spirit showed me that Intention, no matter how far afield we have gone in our soul thoughts and/or feelings, even sin, is a gift the Spirit placed in our new Life when He came in and began to minister Jesus to us.

On the Spirit side, three words describe the activities of the Spirit: Knowing, Loving, Willing. These activities of the Spirit make up what we call Life – Jesus there to do His Life through our spirit knower, lover and willer. When God created Adam, His Spirit had been breathed into the clay He had picked up from the earth He had made and Adam became a living soul. This is the way Adam lived: God's Life being expressed out through Adam's soul. That all changed when Adam and Eve sinned. The Liar who had tempted took over, creating darkness and confusion. Fast forward now to when we knew we needed Jesus and accepted Him. He reclaimed His rightful place in our spirit. As we learn that this has really happened in us and that it is what we want more than our own sorry way, we begin to experience going to Him with questions. As we wait on Him, we begin to get His Knowing: the Spirit pointing out things in His written Word or our hearing bits and pieces from others. One day the Spirit reminds us that He has answered our query and we know with His knowing. Perhaps we are having a heck of a time loving – perhaps members of our family -- and finally the Spirit convinces us that we can't change them or us. The Spirit prompts us to bring it to Him and give the task of loving to Him. Somehow we find Him Loving through us. Our Soul environment has changed. When we are tempted to sin in some way, (real temptation is too strong for us to handle) we want to pour cold water on the temptation. We want to will it out of our minds, but Satan keeps nagging us with justifications. The Willer is there, waiting for us to simply look to Him, ask Him. Satan can't stay when God is in the situation and strangely we find ourselves willing His Will. What I have described is living in His rest. He rested on the seventh day and He has been crooking His finger at His children ever since, saying, in effect, "Here with me in my rest is where your Heart has always yearned to be."

FAITH

As you can see, He directed my attention first to Hebrews 4:12 and gave me some of the understandings I hope have been conveyed to you. One day I seriously read the verse before it: Hebrews 4:11 and found that they really go together. That is why 4:12 begins with "For". 4:11: "Let us labor therefore to enter into that rest, lest any person fall under the same example of unbelief". I saw the word "labor". I was pretty much in favor of the word "rest" and was pondering the Spirit's reason for using the word connoting hard work in the same verse. He was quick to answer. He linked rest to faith, saying that 4:12 was a perfect description of walking in faith. Using the lesson on appearances, He said that turning my back on the appearances of a situation, when all my life until then I have drawn my conclusions from appearances, is a thing I can't do. I thought that strange, but He hurried to remind me that the sword separating appearances and marrow, when some upset appears in my soul, is there so I can see that I am not left alone to solve problems, fix relationships, etc. Faith takes me to the Marrow: His wisdom, love, patience where I find His Way being carried out. The LABOR is ignoring the Liar's chanting, "No. No. No. It won't work. You know it won't work. This is the way you've always done it!!! You know you can't ignore the obvious." Once we have embarked on the way of LIFE, and begin laboring (refusing to listen to the Liar who is making so much sense to our feelings and reasonings) there is this growing pleasure in resting in His rest, trusting His Word, hearing and responding to His Voice. The word "labor" in that verse becomes adventure instead of burdensome work.

I was reminded of C.S. Lewis's story *THE LION, THE WITCH AND THE WARDROBE.* It is a fantasy bearing the truth. One of the children in this charming story is inquiring of Mr. Tumnis about the lion named Aslan (Jesus). He says, "Is Aslan safe?" Mr. Tumnis, a faun, answers "Safe?! NO! Of course He isn't safe. He is good." In effect, when I asked the Spirit of the Living God about the word "labor" in the verse with "rest", he told me that Faith (rest in Him) isn't easy. It is LIFE that we were born looking for.

The environment of the soul is, little by little, changed from that of the turmoil in which Satan hides himself to the rest God planned for us from the very beginning and before.

Laurie is famous for this heart illustration from Hebrews 4:12. Laurie sometimes says that the word "word" here is more about God speaking to us in our hearts than it is about the Bible (often called The Word), though it is applicable there as well. The words (revelations) we hear from God divide our soul and spirit. He takes us through various experiences where we have to rely on Him and not go by appearances.

I like the way Laurie uses the other phrases in these verses to clarify what dividing these two places means. We can see a joint by moving our elbow, wrist, knee, etc. But we cannot see the marrow that is inside the bones. The invisible marrow is the "life" of the bones as Jesus is our life, seen only as He lives out through us. Also, we can have a thought that is very, very different from our intent. Our intent is what we believe, "pushed to the wall," so to speak. I may feel very angry with a loved one, but what would I do if someone were about to harm them? I would die for them. Laurie taught us to live from the invisible life of Christ within, the human spirit in union with the Holy Spirit. Like Dan's above and below the line illustration, we live from what is unseen (marrow, intents) and not from the seen (joints, thoughts.)

FAITH AND COMMUNION

Dan's line and swing illustrations and Laurie's heart illustration help me tremendously as I walk not in the seen and touchable world. Dan's teaching on the Cross explained how union happens and gave clarity to the Lord's Supper or Communion. Dan says there are two sides to the Cross and the two sides correspond to the two symbols of the Lord's Supper. From his book, *The Rest of the Gospel*, I quote:

> There are two sides of the cross. The first is the blood side. That's where Christ died for us. He shed His blood for the forgiveness of our sins. The second side is the body side. We were united with Him on the cross, participating in His death, burial, and resurrection. Our old man was crucified with Him. Our new man, righteous and holy, was resurrected with Him.
>
> These two sides of the cross are not unfamiliar to us. We celebrate them every time we take communion. We eat the bread. We drink the cup. Except most Christians don't have a clue as to what the bread, representing the body, really means. It means that we were united with Him, and when He died, we died. When He was buried, we were buried. When He was raised, we were raised. The heart of Paul's theology is built on the Lord's Supper: the blood and the body. Christ died for us: we died with Him.
>
> We don't feel dead. We don't look dead. We often don't act dead. But at some point the Holy Spirit pulls back the curtain and shows us that in the deepest part of us, our spirit—who we truly are—a death has occurred that has forever changed us. We're going to look the same, feel the same, and think the same on many, many days. But we're going to know something: we're not the same.
>
> In the unseen and eternal realm an exchange has taken place in our spirit that, once we know it, produces through us a quality of life that's different from anything else the world has seen. It's light in darkness. It's other-love in a world of self-love. It's desirable. And it's in us. From Chapter 3, Page 43.

After learning this from Dan, taking communion was never quite the same again. I think about being in Christ there, dying with Him so that I could become a new creation and He can live His life out through me, as me. Thank you, Dan and Laurie for such clarification.

Another of my favorite lesson from Dan is his teaching on Adam and Eve. Since God is the only source of Life in the Universe, then all people are *receivers* of Life. Dan says that makes us all Eves, even the men. We cannot make life, only God can. But we are made to receive life from Him as when a union takes place in marriage and a baby is conceived, the woman receives the life of the man and expresses it to the world. It is not *her life*; it is the man's. Everyone sees her carrying the life.

So it is with us as humans who receive God's life. We express the life we receive, because we cannot make life on our own. And I loved it whenever I heard Dan say with his wonderful smile, "And when there is a union, a conception, the baby WILL come forth!" I was so glad to hear that because it meant to me that someday, people would truly see Jesus in me as I was living and expressing His life. It would come. Satan tries to get us to believe, as he did Adam and Eve, that we can make life on our own. Only God is the Creator of Life.

FAITH AND THE SINGLE EYE

I have mentioned in a place or two another life changing truth from Norman, Dan and Laurie that I would like to elaborate. They call this topic "Living from the single eye." It is a very significant part of how I live to this day. (In a few pages I will tell how Anabel Gillham illustrates this truth with her envelope story.)

The idea of a "single eye" comes from the verses in Matthew 6:22-23, the King James Version. "The light of the body is the eye: if therefore thine eye be single, thy whole body shall be full of light. But if thine eye be evil, thy whole body shall be full of darkness. If therefore the light that is in thee be darkness, how great is that darkness!"

Other versions translate "single" as "healthy," "good," or "clear." I like the word "single" as it helps compare this verse to the one in James 1: 8 about a double minded man being unstable. When seeing life and our circumstances through a "single eye," we see them through our union—we see that God is in every situation and that there is a reason for all we go through. We no longer call situations good or bad. We call them "God" and wait to see what He is going to teach us through them.

If we go back to Genesis 3 and look at the two trees there, we can see another example of double and single that gives us the Biblical basis for seeing situations from God's perspective. God called the tree that Adam and Eve were not supposed to eat from the Tree of the Knowledge of Good and Evil. The other tree in the Garden was the Tree of Life. When we do not live from a "single eye" we see good and bad and live under the Tree of that knowledge. We judge whether something is good or bad by how it looks and feels, by appearances. Sometimes good things feel very painful and bad things feel very pleasurable. Living from the single eye views everything from God's perspective, the Tree of Life.

I could give 100's of examples of seeing God in everything, but let me pick one or two. A few years ago, my friend Margie was buying her first house. She believed that God had shown her the house and wanted her to buy it. A few weeks after beginning the processes, the realtor told Margie there was a problem and she might not get the house. As Margie and I talked about it, I told her that we would not call this "bad" but call it "God " and stand on the fact that she believed He had told her this was to be her house. Eventually, all worked out and she bought the house. Because of this situation, Margie learned to trust God no matter what the appearances looked like and to further know within herself that she had truly heard God directing her.

Have you ever had a terrible blow-up with a loved one? Of course we all have. I recently had one and it felt and looked bad, bad, bad. The pain involved was great because of the rift that came from the exchanged words. I had to call it "God" and not bad, though it looked and felt that way. I knew from experience and from knowing God that He was up to something that I would learn about and/or know differently. After a time of pain and holding on to Him, I saw what I needed to see. Living in the Single Eye did not diminish the pain that I felt, but it did comfort me to know that God was at work even when I did not yet know what He wanted me to get from the situation. This has proven to be a life-changing truth through the years since I heard it from Dan and Laurie.

Dan says in *The Rest of the Gospel,* that God uses the uncomfortable or negative situations that come our way to get our attention. We don't usually stop and focus on the pleasant ones. When we stop in our tracks because of the negative, we have to exercise faith to look past it and see that God is at work no matter how it looks and feels. In our spirit union with God we see Him as the source and Him as the solution. "Nothing happens in our lives for which there is not a God reason." (pp. 132-133)

"But what about evil?" we want to ask. Dan explains that it doesn't matter so much who causes something (Satan or God) as it matters how we take it into ourselves. Positive results come from seeing it as from God. Negative results come from seeing the cause as Satan or some other person. Satan and evil are real and sometimes have to be dealt with, but on another level we go beyond that and talk about our situations as Jesus did when he called his crucifixion, "the *Father's* cup." In Genesis 50:20, Joseph tells his brothers, "You meant it for evil, but God meant it for good." That is a single eye.

Dan sums it up very well: "God is not the author of evil, but in His sovereignty He uses even evil to accomplish His purposes in us and in the world. Sometimes I use the expression, 'He's in it, and He means it, but it's not His righteousness. . . God is in everything, and God means everything, but everything is not God." (pp. 134-136)

A Biblical example of what Dan is saying takes place in 1 Kings 18. Elijah had just defeated the prophets of Baal and shown them the power of the true God. Then he ran away depressed. God told Elijah that He was going to pass by and Elijah experienced an earthquake, wind and fire. God was in them, but not in them; He brought them, but 1 Kings says, "God was not in them." Then God came to Elijah and he heard a "still small voice." Dan summarizes this paradox by paraphrasing God, "Everything of your life is ultimately me, Elijah. I've set the whole thing in motion and nothing happens which I am not active in. I take the messes and change them into discipline or blessing. I'm part of the outer things in your life and I use them. They are not the deepest understanding of Me you can have. You are going to miss Me if that is the deepest you can go." (Paraphrased from p. 76, *The Rest of the Gospel*)

As I walk through my journey of faith and take the negatives that happen as coming ultimately from God, the peace that I experience is definitely beyond understanding. There may be pain, suffering and sadness, but He shows Himself as faithful and I always learn something new.

FAITH AND EXPRESSIONS

As I was learning all these new ways to think about my Christian walk, I found the same question continually arose in my mind: "Well, what does it really mean for someone to see Jesus in me? " Unknown to me, I had always believed, that Jesus would most likely look perfect, always kind of sweet, never upset and always doing ministry or praying or reading the Bible. My thoughts usually went something like this: "This certainly will never be reachable for me in this lifetime. I am not the sweetest person around and everyone knows that I am not perfect. I do read my Bible and pray a lot, but I still get upset. Oh, yes, I do serve a lot, too, but are the motives pure?" Around and around I would go, comparing my behavior and feelings to whatever this picture was that I had of "being like Jesus."

I had other questions nagging at me. Who is "me?' How do the negatives in my actions and attitudes fit in if part of me is holy, righteous and blameless, but I still act badly sometimes? What do I do with things about me that I don't like? If I am already like Jesus in my spirit, then what is it that really changes when I change? These questions were slowly getting answers and words in which to put the answers. Sometimes it was very difficult to share these new ideas. (In the section about Jewels from JW, I will talk at length about learning more about "who is me?")

What a relief to learn early on with Dr. Solomon that I was accepted in the Beloved (Ephesians 1:6b). That helped tremendously to ease the burden of performing for acceptance. But I had even greater relief when I understood the soul and spirit division. Since my husband and I were teaching these ideas to others in a small group, finding words and illustrations were very helpful for clarifying union and walking in the Spirit: Here are three examples that answered some of my questions:

THE CANDLEHOLDER: A candleholder is made of three parts, like we are. There is the candleholder itself, which is sometimes plain, sometimes beautiful, sometimes ordinary, sometimes it is even ornate. Then there is the candle. The candle (our soul) sits inside the candleholder (our body). Each candleholder is different. Each candle is different. But there is one thing that is the same—the flame. The light is Jesus in union with our human spirit. When he shines through the candleholder, the light looks different, glowing and flickering through each holder in a unique way. We can see this in a room full of lit candles. The holders can be different colors, shapes, and designs, flickering in different shapes and making various shadows. But the flame is the same. Jesus is going to appear differently living through each person, while at the same time He will be like Himself, as we know Him and His characteristics from the Bible. I came to rest in knowing He would look different through each person's unique personality and body and that there was not anything wrong with me if I did not fit into some pre-conceived idea of what He should look like. No body type or personality is better or worse than another. When the flame is lit (and it never goes out by the way), He is living, living as me. John 8:12 says, "Again, therefore Jesus spoke to them, saying, '*I* am the light of the world . . .'" Then in Matthew 5:14 as Jesus is teaching He says to the multitudes, "*You* are the light of the world . . .." (Italics mine) This sounds like the two are one to me.

THE DENTED TUBE: This illustration comes from my second son, Bob. He was just a teenager when we were learning these truths and his youthful zeal, teachability and faith helped me all the time! What a joy to see a young and uncluttered life be able to explain things of the Lord. His version of growing and changing, though we are already perfect in our spirit, goes something like this.

Our life is like a dented tube. The dents are negatives, qualities, habits, etc., that are part of our lives that don't match how God would like us to appear or act. Inside the tube is Jesus, in union with us. It is His job to take care of the dents. He will punch out the dents when and as HE sees fit. Sometimes we can help and other times we cannot, but we can always co-operate. It is up to Him which dents get "worked on," and when. As we notice other people's dents, we don't try to undent them or tell Jesus when and what to do with them. He accepts us with our dents and we accept others with their dents, waiting and co-operating as He fixes dents in His time. We can pray for others' dents, but love them where they are, as Jesus loves us where we are.

WASHING DISHES AND CHANGING DIAPERS: This illustration came to my mind as I often interacted with young mothers who were extremely busy with small children and running their households. It could be very difficult for them to have a time alone for prayer and Bible study. Through the years of mentoring various busy mothers, I often heard their longing for *any kind* of private time and their guilt over little time for concentrated prayer and study. As I began to understand union and how knowing that could affect my prayer life, it became clearer to me that my life, my living and breathing, was actually prayer. That helped me understand for the first time how one could "Pray without ceasing" (I Thessalonians 5: 17). I had read the book about Brother Lawrence who prayed without ceasing as he worked in the kitchen of his monastery. It puzzled me until I understood my union with Christ. Since He is my life, then my life is prayer. Since there is no separation between us, then whatever I am doing (that is not the once and a while sin) is Him doing it.

These things, along with removing guilt and condemnation from their lives, were what I wanted others to know. Whatever we, in union with Christ, are doing, it is Christ living in and through us doing it. If we are washing dishes, Jesus is living through us, washing the dishes. If we are changing diapers, it is Jesus doing it. (Galatians 2:20) He is our very life (Colossians 3:4) and there is no "ordinary" thing that is too insignificant for Him to be in us and do through us. In truth there is no secular or spiritual where Christ is living.

Because we have been taught so deeply that there is a division between secular and spiritual things, we tend to think that Jesus is only in and through us during things we are used to calling "spiritual," like reading the Bible, praying, witnessing, going to church. This separation carries over to the working place, which I think discourages us from looking like a Christian when out in the world. There *is* a difference in worldliness and spirituality, but for me there is no so-called "secular." Jesus is about ordinary living and wants to appear through us wherever we are. There *is* a place for concentrated study and prayer, but we do not have to sit down in a certain place, at a certain time to ceaselessly talk with the One who is never away from us. The "do" is more about remembering that we are One with the God of the Universe and He is using our hands to change diapers, run a computer or to build a building.

FAITH AND WARFARE

Growing up and as an adult Christian, the circles in which I moved were very quiet about Spiritual warfare. During these years of new awareness, I first learned how Satan lies to us about who we are and tries to keep us from knowing deeply how much we are loved and accepted. He wants us to continue believing all the old messages that were "programmed" into our minds as we grew up. Even in great families, children learn wrong believing about themselves, God, and life.

One thing that helped me stop listening to lies, was when I heard Dr. Bill Gillham say that Satan usually speaks to us in First Person Singular, or with "I." In our minds, we hear these lies as "I can't do anything right. I'm ugly, I'm stupid, I'm clumsy, etc." He says that hearing it this way makes us think it is our thoughts and thus they must be true. I began to realize, the more I understood oneness with Christ, that to an extent there were only "two voices" I would hear in my mind—God's and Satan's. God's voice, which also often spoke with "I," would say truth, unconditional love, acceptance, faith, and other Godly words. Satan's voice might sound good and sound like me by using first person singular, but what I was hearing would be lies, selfishness, doubt, fear, condemnation, etc. Anything that was of the flesh or world would go on the Satan side.

These clues were very helpful. While reading the biography about Reese Howells, the great intercessor in Wales before and during World War II, I read that someone once asked him, "How do you know God's voice so well?" Mr. Howells came back with a statement that pierced my heart when I read it, "You know your mother's voice when she calls, don't you?" I remember whispering softly to the Lord Jesus, "Of course I know my mother's voice. I don't have to ask her who she is. I want to know you like that." The ability to distinguish God's voice grew and better filled some of that deep longing I'd always had to know Him.

Coupled with understanding Satan's lies and my son Bob's dented tube illustration, I began to see the answers to one of my other questions, "What is it exactly that changes when we grow?" It is a given fact in the world (supported by Scripture in Mathew 12: 34, 35) that we live out of what we believe. We can say one thing and live another. We can have knowledge in our head and not live it out. We live out *what we truly believe on a deep level.* So I began to see the importance of lies and truth and helping people realize what they are actually believing, because what changes is not "the bad me." There is no longer a bad me. That is already changed because I am a new creation where the real me is united with Jesus. What changes is what I believe!

Many times we are taught to try to change behavior so that we will be a better person. But our behavior comes from what we are believing and changes as we take the new or truthful believing and live from it. This is how we can say, "There is 'nothing' wrong with me." This is why we can say, "I accept myself and others no matter what." The thing that is "wrong" is our believing! That believing changes as we take by faith what God says and reject what the enemy of our souls says. Depending on the issue, behavior will change immediately or slowly. This is why we can take our focus off of behavior as the standard for accepting ourselves or another person. We can take our focus off of sin and believe that we will sin less in doing so.

Getting the answer to what changes flipped Galatians 5:16 right side up for me. For many years and from ideas that crept through in teaching I received, I unknowingly heard and believed that verse to be saying, "If you do not carry out the desires of the flesh, (do the do's and don't do the don'ts) then you will walk in the Spirit." This is not what the verse says. It says, "But I say, walk by the Spirit and you will not fulfill the desires of the flesh." That's a very big difference. The monkey was taken off of my back to perform. My walking, my behavior would change when my believing lined up with God's truth. This was backwards to the ideas that permeated some teachings that told me I had to perform a certain way to be righteous and a good Christian.

It was very freeing as I began to stop listening to "old messages" in my head and began to say the truth to myself *even if I did not feel it or see it.* Many things changed in my prayer life, my relationships and my ministry. But I had not seen the whole truth about warfare with Satan and how his voice could affect us. I had always been taught and believed that a Christian could not have a demon. I was soon to add demonic activity to my list of "Satan's voices."

At a conference in 1993, God used Dr. Charles Kraft and Dr. E. James Wilder (this is JW of the Jewels fame with more later from him) to show me a larger picture of demonology and the spiritual realm. Dr. Kraft, a leading author and speaker on this topic, makes it very clear that the Scriptures should not be translated, "possessed" when speaking of demons and Christians, but that the word means, "have." He explains that demons can be in a Christian, in their body or soul, but not in their spirit, which is where Jesus lives. He teaches a very clear way to handle deliverance without fanfare and chaos. (See Dr. Kraft's book *Defeating Dark Angels* for further study). We know that the Enemy is defeated and we stand on that without fear.

As I learned and began to do prayer ministry for warfare, I saw God's power in a new way and my faith grew stronger as I saw Him free people from generational sin, oppression from past abuse, evil influences, lies and every-day harassment. There is nothing to fear from demons, their voices and activities, but I came to see that they are a real factor in our walk of victory.

FAITH AND LOVE

As I settled in to my new walk, I could see God slowly changing how I loved people, because now I was loving myself based on how He saw me. It was easier to see others and myself like God does—loving us exactly where we are, while at the same time seeing us where we can be. Yes, we are acceptable, loved, worthy, awesome creations, but He does want us to grow to experience all those attributes, showing them on the outside. There were many, many times that I had to remind myself that who I (or the other) am and what I (or the other) do are two very different things.

In our world, we are taught the opposite of this everywhere. It is pounded into us from the crib. If we act badly, we are bad. If we act nicely, we are good girls and boys. Then we turn around and call ourselves and each other good or bad based mainly on behavior. Most of the time we reject whatever we consider bad. That rejection can take many forms-- from things such as simple anger to verbal or other forms of abuse, phoniness in relationships or withdrawing our love in some form. God tells us that we are not good or bad by what we do, but because of Who we have as our life. If one is not a Christian and does not have Christ, then he is bad even if he does great and glorious good works. If one has Christ, he is essentially good in his personhood, even if he sins once and a while.

Coming to deeply understand and practice this new way of believing was a slow but sure process. I wanted to love with God's love, both people easy to love and people difficult to love. Isn't God's kind of love "the greatest of these?" (1 Corinthians 13) As the knowledge that I was really and truly one with Christ deepened in my heart, unconditional love grew and became more and more experiential in my life. This kind of love is hard to put into words, but I think it has to do with not looking on the outside at how a person acts, but rather seeing the person's heart, who they are, in spite of their words and actions. This goes for non-believers as well. We can see their personhood as it is or will be through Heaven's eyes.

It feels strange sometimes to love someone who is acting badly and perhaps not even being able to speak to them about their actions. It can look like condoning the actions, but only God can show us when to confront. The same way "whatever means whatever" with faith, "unconditional means unconditional" with love—no matter what.

Many times as I have loved someone (not a child) who is acting badly, I've been led to say to them *one time* that I did not like the behavior. Most people that know us well know what we approve and disapprove of anyway. Saying it once was all, as I continued loving no matter what. Other times God would not let me say anything. He decides. Because of Adam and Eve deciding that *they* would decide what is good and bad, we cannot always trust what we observe and think is bad. Of course some things are black and white in the Scriptures, but even then, we are not to be someone's Holy Spirit. (Speaking to someone about hurting us with their words or actions is another topic altogether.)

For several years I have been involved with deeply wounded people as a counselor or close friend, and it has become evident to me that nearly all forms of negative behavior come from people's painful, unhealed wounds. Without unconditional love and joy in their lives there is nothing for them to draw upon for living well. Without safety and acceptance, they can find no one to trust. When I was able to be on the inside of wounded people's lives and see how horrible it was to feel completely unloved, unworthy and hopeless, it became easier to overlook negative behavior. Unconditional love is everyone's need and giving it changes the giver and the receiver.

FAITH AND FORGIVENESS

Unlike some of my beliefs, what I believed about the subject of forgiveness was an area that did not change drastically over the years. I think it must have been a part of my character from early years and was not a difficult thing for me to do. I have never been a "grudge holder." After attending a seminar by Bill Gothard in the mid '70's, I adopted and taught my children to use the words he suggests for a clear apology: "I was wrong to ______, will you forgive me?" It made sense to me that asking that question gives the offended person the chance to say, "Yes" or "No." If we only say, "I'm sorry," the other is left with the choice of saying, "It's okay," (which is usually not true) or saying nothing at all, just acting like it never happened. It takes much more humility to say, "I was wrong, will you forgive me?"

The expansion about forgiveness that came for me in the '80's was about the concept of forgiving past offenses done to me by someone who might be dead or that I might not want to speak to about their offense. A good friend, Duane Farmer taught us how much energy it uses in one's life when there is unforgiveness in the heart. It can zap daily energy and cause bitterness to grow. (Ephesians 4:31, 32 and Hebrews12: 15) Then he explained an exercise that one can do by faith. It is commonly used these days, but was new to me then. I can picture the person who has offended me sitting in a chair in the room with me. I have found that it helps even more to have a safe, other person there in the room to listen and guide if needed. I can say all the things I would like to say to the one in the chair, however I need to say it. When I am finished, I choose to forgive and say, "I forgive you."

Forgiveness is for us, not always for the offender. It frees us and helps us avoid that root of bitterness. It does not mean that we condone in any way what the person has done to us. It does not mean that we forget what they did. But what it does mean is that the offense becomes less intrusive and less sharp in our mind. It also means that now I have given up the right to hold it against them and, as Duane put it, the account I have with them is at zero. Then I choose to keep their account at zero, not allowing offenses to pile up unforgiven. This has nothing to do with confronting the person, nor does it mean I will have a close relationship with them if they are some kind of danger to me.

When I began to counsel deeply wounded people, I learned another aspect of forgiveness: that no one should be pressured to hurry and forgive too soon. People need time to recognize and feel anger, sadness, fear or other feelings connected to the offenses. Forgiveness must not be a band-aid or a quick fix. It can take time for a person to come to a place of forgiveness. There are situations when one may not be able to confront an offender, but with love and help from God and a safe person, it is possible to forgive by faith.

FAITH AND CONFRONTATION

Sometimes when I have been offended, I need to talk to the offender. This is a delicate issue and must be approached with much prayer and thoughtful pondering. Most of us are very fearful about confrontation. It is easier when both persons can approach the issue maturely. I usually go by how easy the offense is to let go of and forget without confronting. If it continues to eat at me or I am putting up a wall towards the other person, then I know I need to talk. If I sense that someone has put up a wall towards me, I like to ask them about that as well. Maybe I have offended them unknowingly. Faith is part of this process here because we have to trust God with the courage to confront and be willing to have some upset during the process. It is worth the upset to be reconciled and have all walls taken down. It is even better to deal with the bricks before they become a wall.

FAITH AND TRIALS

During difficult times, it can take all the strength we have to cling to God and believe that He is in control and has not left us. He tells us in Hebrews 13:5, "I will never leave you nor forsake you." The degree to which we cling to God in trying or painful times is related to how well we already know Him, how well we have learned to know and trust "the ice." Each trial has the potential to deepen our knowledge of God and His love and trustworthiness. We can choose to turn our back on Him and believe that He is punishing us or does not love us. Or, we can choose to believe what the Bible tells us about His character and that He never does anything that is not love. 1 John 4:8b tells us "God is love." We read in Titus 1:2 that "God cannot lie," and in Romans 8:28 that "All things work together for good for those who love God and are called according to His purpose." These three verses alone are a general idea of who God is and very helpful in keeping our hearts clinging to Him in times of trouble.

Being angry with God for a season during a trial is not the same as turning from Him. He can handle our anger and indeed welcomes the honesty. I did not learn in my early life that it was all right to be that honest with God. Somewhere along the way, I learned that it was not "spiritual" to feel angry with others and certainly not with God. One day after a series of broken down cars that left one or all of our family stranded on the highway, I was alone in my bedroom, kneeling by the bed. I screamed at God, "Why? Why? Why do you keep doing this? No wonder you don't have many followers! Look how you treat the ones you do have!" I felt so frustrated and angry that we kept having car problems. I did know enough to know God was in control and nothing comes into my life that He does not allow, thus seeing Him in the situations. But I still felt very frustrated and wanted it to stop happening.

Anabel Gillham's explanation of John 14: 20, ("In that day, you shall know that I am in the Father, and you in Me and I in You") had been a big help in seeing God in such situations. She likened this verse to a bunch of envelopes and tells it like this in her book, *The Confident Woman*, page 95:

> Go get three envelopes of graduated sizes and a small slip of paper. Now, on the largest of the envelopes, print GOD. On the next size down, print JESUS. On the smallest of the three, print your name. On your slip of paper, print Jesus. Now take your large GOD envelope and place your JESUS envelope inside it. Take the envelope with your name on it and place it inside the JESUS envelope. Now take the slip of paper with Jesus printed on it and drop it into the envelope with your name on it. 'When I come back to life again, you shall know that I am in the Father, and you in Me.'
>
> Anything that comes into my life must come through God, through Jesus, to get to me; and when it gets there it finds me filled with Jesus, so what is there to fear?

This was what I was trying to hold onto as I knelt by my bed in frustration. But at the same time I was tired of so many aggravating circumstances. I yelled at God a few more times. No lightening bolts came through the ceiling nor did any harsh voices resound through the room. I laid my head down on the bed. I felt a sense of relief and peace that God could handle me being angry with Him. He did not condemn nor did He punish. But neither did He relieve the trials.

The trials hardly let up for the next ten to fifteen years. They came in various forms and degrees both large and small. But in the trials, by faith as I clung to the truth, verses such as James 1:1 and 2 became real in my experience, not just in my head. "Consider it all joy my brethren, when you encounter various trials, knowing that the testing (proving) of your faith produces endurance, and let endurance have its perfect result that you may be perfect and complete, lacking in nothing." As I Peter 1: 6 and 7 say, ". . . you have been distressed by various trials, that the proof of your faith, being more precious than gold, . . . may be found to result in praise and glory and honor at the revelation of Jesus Christ."

Trials are the very tool that God uses to prove our faith. He knows what we want and long for and slowly builds that into our experience. He knows when it will take trials and when it will take blessings, and uses both. As the engineer of our faith, God already knows how we will stand, the same way a bridge engineer knows that the bridge he is designing will hold up all the cars that pass over it. He does not *test* the bridge before it opens for use; he *proves* what he already knew it would do.

There are degrees of trials, of course. Broken down cars have little comparison to losing a loved one, getting a divorce, or being told someone has cancer. The pain involved can be very severe and extremely difficult to feel. But the same God and the same faith will carry us through. He will understand and accept all our feelings without condemnation or surprise. David puts it well in Psalm 130: 1 "Out of the depths, I have cried to Thee, O Lord." He continues in verse 5, "I wait for the Lord, my soul does wait; And in His word do I hope." When I found myself in the depths of despair, pain, and hopelessness, the only thing I could do was to wait for the Lord and hope in His word. For me, that not only meant His words from my Bible, but His words in my heart or from the mouths of safe and caring others.

Remember, "The better we know the ice (God), the more we will trust it (Him)." God wants us to say what He says about trials, no matter the intensity. He wants us to look to Him and cling to His goodness, His grace and His love. He can handle any feelings we have and longs for us to express them to Him—then cry out to Him in faith that He is the answer to whatever is going on.

FAITH AND PARENTING

I think that rearing children is the most blessed and most difficult thing in the world to do. Children are valuable and precious. Little is more important than the privilege of "molding" a person for the future. This task ought to be one of our top priorities, not something that we do in left over time. Good parenting will be another book in itself, but I would speak a moment to where faith comes in to this issue.

I cannot imagine how difficult it must be to try parenting without God. For me it was one of my greatest daily faith builders, as well as moment-by-moment character growing in my own life. My four children are all married with children of their own now and being their parent and the grandmother to their children has been one of my greatest blessings.

I knew that day that I committed my life to Christ to be a Christian wife and mother that it was one of my deep desires to have and rear Godly children. Like many of us, I had no idea what being a good mother meant exactly, Christian or otherwise. So I set out to find that path as many ways as possible. I read books and magazines about parenting. I read the book of Proverbs over and over. During the years with Campus Crusade, I went to many seminars and had wise teachers that helped me with parenting ideas and tips. It was there that I learned that I could "disciple" (now called mentoring) my children. We were encouraged to have another adult or two we were mentoring, but that our children were our "first disciples." Moses tells us in Deuteronomy 6:4-9 that we "shall teach them (the words in verses 4 and 5) diligently to your sons and shall talk of them when you sit in your house and when you walk by the way and when you lie down and when you rise up" (verse 7).

For me this verse meant that I would teach my children about God all the time, in every day events, using problems, hurts, mistakes to bring Him into the picture. I wanted them to grow to be independent of us as their parents into being dependent on God. I wanted them to follow God and His ways, to be honest and trustworthy with good character. I wanted them to love others and be kind to "outcasts" around them. I wanted them to be good citizens who knew how to keep a job and work well at whatever that job was. I wanted them to know how to handle their money and not be extremely materialistic. I wanted them to learn consequences of their behavior and not bail them out of those consequences, as they grew older.

These ideas make a small list of all that goes into "molding" a child. It is a long and very slow process that is made up of many moments and days. Faith spoke loudly that I could not do this without God, nor could I lead them in anything that I did not have in my own life. "More is caught than taught," we heard often. I had to trust God with every aspect of my life and theirs. When it did not look like the attributes and qualities were there that I wanted for them, I had to believe that God was working in their lives anyway and had them in His hands.

During my children's early childhood, I had a *little* control of their environments, (I emphasize "little" because we really have far less control than we think) but as they grew to teens, I had to let go more and more and cling to God with my mouth shut except in prayer. By college years, I knew that they could basically do whatever they wanted while away from home. My place was to love unconditionally, supporting them but not condoning behavior I did not agree with, accepting who they are, however that was being played out, and leave them in God's hands.

Trusting God with my parenting, with my children, was one of the hardest and biggest steps of faith in my life. It meant that I had to watch them go through difficulties and love them right where they were, while God taught them lessons that only He could teach. I could pray and cry out to God, but I could not interfere. There was no going back to those formative years where I had some control. There was only faith that God would keep His promise that if I "trained up a child in the way he should go, when he was old, he would not depart from it." (Proverbs 22:6.) As one teacher told me, there was an important phrase in this verse—"in the way <u>he</u> should go." This means that as we train children, each one's individual needs must be taken into account. Some things we do and teach will be universal, like teaching them not to lie, steal, etc., but other aspects will be about their individual personalities, personal desires, talents and skills. This helped me be able to accept my children more unconditionally and not compare them as much with one another.

Currently I live with four of my grandchildren. This is one of my greatest privileges and joys. God is allowing me the honor of a "second chance," so to speak, of parenting, since I am with these four little ones so much. I feel the sorrow that comes with retrospect when I see my immaturity, of things I did not do well with my own four. I feel the regret of the things I did not know or that had not matured in me while rearing them. But I do not linger on the regrets since they cannot be changed. Instead I get to love my grandchildren, all of them, with a more mature and joy-filled love.

It seems a big part of who I am is to love and be comfortable with children. There never was a year without one around, even if not my own. To be able to have a small part of influencing the next generation is too wonderful to describe. I get to watch another bunch grow and learn and mature. I am more patient with them because I am more mature. I play and laugh with them and sometimes spoil them. But living with them brings the necessity of disciplining sometimes as well. This keeps me on my toes and aware of any anger or impatience that wants to rise up. Being with children is like that. They are a moment-by-moment faith tonic for anyone who wishes to partake of it and not run away from it. I thank God every day for all He has taught and is teaching me about children—and about relating--as I learn from them.

FAITH AND JOY

We are creatures of joy and born to live in it. My journey of faith has taken me through many trials and sufferings that did not feel very joyful. Through some of them, I met a man of joy who has mentored me the last several years. He knows suffering and does it well because he also knows very well how joy works in our lives. It has been my privilege to grow in faith as this man taught me how to live in joy. He helped me know myself better and find the depths of my new name, Bringer of Joy. That first day that God asked me to sign my name as BOJ, I had to make myself do it. Most of the time now, I accept and live in that as who I am. Now and then, I struggle with believing it, but the journey of faith is easier now and the struggles do not last more than a few minutes. I do not act perfectly all the time, nor do I always have a great attitude, but I want to say that there is hope that the truths we take by faith will definitely take us. There is a seeing and experiencing of "those things we hoped for and the evidence of those things not seen" in the early years of our journey. Joy does come in the morning as we walk by faith that Jesus is our Joy.

Joy means, "Someone is glad to be with me, no matter what." It is true that even when forsaken by all humans, Jesus is glad to be with us and that is very comforting. But what I desire to remember each day is that people need other people to be glad to be with them as well. We all need to be the sparkle in someone's eye and see them light up to see us. So now, by faith, I live that I am here to bring joy to those around me, by being glad to be with them, no matter what. In and through me, Jesus will fill their joy buckets so that they can suffer well and keep the faith as He brings all of us along in our journey of faith.

But there was a time when I forgot about joy. My joy bucket was completely empty and dry, clouded by depression. My marriage was failing and that trauma from the past haunted me, its pain lying deeply buried and affecting even the joy I'd found in knowing freedom in Christ. In the '80's I had worked on this event as Jim and I had learned to counsel and to teach the Exchanged Life. I thought it was finished and healed. But there remained a portion untouched, waiting on God's timing. There were more things I must learn before God could heal that untouched portion. In that deeply buried place of pain there was a treasure chest just waiting to be rediscovered and filled with jewels. God would be the refiner and JW would give the jewels until I, myself, became the jewel refined.

PART TWO

JEWELS FROM JW

INTRODUCTION

In Part One of my journey, I purposely left out any details about the trauma in my life and the divorce that came after almost 34 years of marriage. By 1993 my life had changed so drastically that it seemed as if I were not living my own life. There was little joy left by the end of that year.

As I share details in Part Two, there may be a bit of repetition as I tie the two journeys together. Hopefully that will just be helpful and not a hindrance to the reader. I will be sharing from letters and phone calls that I had with Dr. E. James Wilder (JW), author of *The Stages of a Man's Life, The Red Dragon Cast Down,* co-author of *The Life Model, Living From the Heart Jesus Gave You* and *Living with Men.*

Jim (JW) lives in California and for the eight years he was my mentor and counselor, we hardly saw each other face to face. Sometimes it was difficult not being able to see his face, but now I can see that it was a blessing. I recently realized that, had we been face to face, I would not have written down almost every word he said to me. I am thankful that I did write in my journals while we talked, so that now I can share the jewels he dropped in my treasure chest.

I now know that God had everything planned out and timed for me to finish processing the buried, unresolved pain from the past that was yet hidden from the trauma I'd had at fourteen. Through the healing process with God and JW, I would rediscover a lost part of myself. That rediscovery would bring me to a deeper understanding of who God created me to be, expanding the understanding of identity I'd learned from the exchanged life and union in Christ teachers. Though the memories of the trauma remained in the background of my journey of faith, I thought I had settled the effects of the trauma in the 1980's. But a piece of it had gone untouched and, especially, unfelt.

I believe God brought JW to help me. He knew things that neither I nor anyone else I knew understood. Some of what I heard personally from JW comes from the books by him listed above. I highly recommend them for further study of the principles he so wonderfully shared with me. If I make a direct quote from any of these works, it will be noted. Otherwise the information was given to me personally.

Although I had been a Christian for many years and a counselor who tried to help others in deep pain, this journey with JW forever changed me more than anything else I have ever been through. Facing my own deeply buried emotional pain taught me first hand how wrongly most of us view pain when we encounter it, either in ourselves or in others. Going back to this painful, buried event brought deep healing, but only after my whole life turned upside down. I want to share this part of my journey as an example of God's faithfulness, love and mercy in hopes that it will help others who might need to undergo such a life changing transformation. I pray also that other counselors might benefit in order to better help those with whom they work and long to bring to healing.

HELPS FOR THE READER

Some Definitions

Nature and Flesh: As I have shared in Part One, my faith journey grew stronger after learning what I call "The Exchanged Life." None of those beliefs changed as I spent time with JW, though his uses of some words gave the beliefs clearer meanings. For the sections following, I would like to reiterate that I do believe that even though Christians do not have the old man, the old self, the old nature (*anthropos* in the Greek), we do still have a condition that JW will call the *sarx* or *sark* (Greek term) or the "picker" (JW's word) and that most translations of the Bible call *the flesh*. Please note that in some passages in some translations of the Bible, the word *sin nature* is used for *sarx*. This can be misleading with the word "nature" there as most people associate "nature" with the words translated from *anthropos*. It is easier to understand the distinctions here when keeping in mind that nature and flesh are two different words in the Greek. It is important to me and my story that these distinctions be made.

The Heart. Another word that can be confusing is the word *heart.* JW's use of the word *heart* is about the new heart that Jesus gives to believers (Ezekiel 36:25-27). I also call it the spirit, the human spirit joined to the Holy Spirit or the real me in union with Jesus.

Hurt and Harm: I would also like to distinguish between the words *hurt* and *harm* in order to make some of the jewels more understandable. Hurt will mean either emotional pain inside a person or something that we do to each other that is not considered abusive. Harm will refer to the idea of abuse that is to be avoided. Because JW and I did not distinguish always with the two words, but knew the meanings we were discussing, *hurt* will sometimes be used for both meanings, as well as meaning *pain.*

The use of the word *pain* will be principally that of emotional pain.

The Fall of Man: What happened? JW describes it this way, "We lost what we had in the garden, our heart (the ability to discern God), and we lost God's words (the ability to communicate directly with Him.) We got the picker instead, which tells us falsely that **we** can discern what is good and evil now. The Greek word for the picker is s*arx.* The Bible word is *Flesh.* After Jesus came and after we receive Him, we get a new heart and the Holy Spirit brings God's words back. Our new heart is always like His. It is the place we discern Him and His will. We cannot listen to the picker because it always lies." (Galatians 5:16-18, Romans 8:5-9 NASB. [Please note the use of the words 'according to the flesh' and 'in the flesh' in this Romans passage])

Redemption, JW's definition: " Redemption is what God does, His part, along with salvation and healing. It's how he takes the garbage of our lives and makes something good out of it. How does God do this? We tell Him how bad it is and ask Him to make something out of it. It is not like denial. Something wonderful is actually happening out of it. *What* is up to Him. God doesn't do maturity, that's our part, and we don't do redemption. When we ask God to redeem us, others who were involved may be very upset by our redemption, if they didn't ask also. So many are afraid to look at the past because it hurts, but we have to see and say how bad it was. God's love is bigger than the fear of looking."

Bonds: Our bonds with other people are emotional connections. (Some authors call this "attachment"). * *The Red Dragon, p. 122*

Spiritual Adoption: When a wounded person is in need of "re-parenting" or has other needs of family interaction bonds, then Spiritual

Adoption can take place. "This is an eternal family bond that changes the family structure permanently for parent, adopted child, brother or sister and for other family members. This bond can only be created by God and must be undertaken only under the guidance of the Holy Spirit." * *The Red Dragon, p. 320*

Knowing What Satisfies: This means that a person knows the important things about life and how to live in them. JW says that, "Receiving and giving life is what satisfies." Others might call it "doing things God's way." Also there is a meaning to it for each individual—the unique things that give them joy—like loving nature, watching children, helping others, etc.

A BRIEF SUMMARY OF THE MATURITY STAGES FROM "THE LIFE MODEL"

Because I will be describing my healing journey with much of JW's terminology, it is important to have an understanding of his levels of maturity in *The Life Model.* These levels are emotionally and task oriented, though ideally they should take place at the correct chronological period. We cannot skip a level and if the next level does not take place at the correct period, the person will be "stuck" emotionally. Therefore, a person's emotional maturity level may not correspond to his or her physical age. Because of my sexual trauma and the resulting pain involved, I was in some ways "stuck" emotionally at the age of fourteen. This will become clearer as the story unfolds.

When we mature into the next level, we take with us all that we learned in any previous levels, adding to them any new tasks and needs. Moving from one level to the next constitutes an identity change. It can be quite significant.

Maturity levels have NOTHING to do with a person's value. We are always valuable no matter our level of maturity. *Earned maturity* is another word for the level one has reached emotionally that has nothing to do with one's age.

THE LEVELS OF MATURITY

Infant: Birth until four years-- principally with mother. Receives without giving. Takes in all he or she needs. Knows how to receive. All of life is about consuming.

Child: Age four until thirteen-- goes out more into the father's world. Can take care of self only. Good at taking care of self. Beginning to know what satisfies. Finds it difficult to take care of others.

Adult: Age thirteen until birth of first child--Can take care of two or more at the same time, with both being satisfied. Time for marriage, not easy, can compromise, knows they are part of history and have an impact on the world. "You can tell the difference in a man and a boy by what they do in the back seat of a car when a teenager. Do they know the effect their behavior has on history?"

Parent: Birth of first child to last child leaving home—Gives without receiving in return. Loves to give what the child cannot give back. It is better to give than receive.

Elder-- Last child gone from home. Ready to parent others who need it; helps the community. (Not to be confused with the chosen or elected office in a church)

Keeping the maturity stages in mind helps us better understand what is happening in an identity change or deep healing as we move to another level. That move can be the normal chronological changes that are supposed to take place naturally or the move can be a result of healing. The identity change that I went through and describe here will be from deep healing.

I have found knowing the levels to be very helpful in relationships as well. I can understand where someone is and accept them there, while seeing where they might need to grow. It lessens judgment because maturity does not have anything to do with value. Maturity is just a fact.

I believe that God sees us complete in Christ, while at the same time He sees where we need to grow. There is no condemnation if a person is not as mature as his or her chronological age. It just means that emotional growth was stunted somewhere and healing is needed. Here are two examples from

JW that help me look at situations differently since I learned the maturity levels:

"If someone thinks they have to take sides in a conflict, that is the child level of maturity."

"The stages of life applied to marriage conflict can be seen this way: If one or both of the spouses think that to settle a conflict each gets half and gives up half, they are in the child stage. If they are adults the thinking will be, 'We will find a way to take care of both of us simultaneously.'"

Young Christians or people with Infant or Child level maturity in their growth must be treated with care. Harm can come from using the "jewels" here unwisely. It is our desire that they be taken as ways to ponder our great God and how He wants to grow us and not be used to insult people that need to mature.

JEWELS FROM JW

Jewels are the precious stones from which we make beautiful, valuable, and sometimes priceless works of art. All around the world jewels are valued by every culture. The "jewels" I received from JW were words and ideas that helped change me into a work of art more fit for the Master's use. These jewels changed my view of pain, strengthened my view of God and settled deep issues from my past. I myself am, also, the Jewel of my Lord Jesus, and just as valuable jewelry is always formed through purification with fire or with cutting tools, just such a refining process filled my treasure box with love and self-esteem. But in order to share these jewels, I must continue my story of the faith journey that brought me to them

Three intricately entwined events shaped my life more than any others. These were not events that came from my faith, but were brought to me by the hand of God in His sovereignty. The first event happened when I was fourteen. I was sexually abused, now known as "date raped." Though I did not know it at the time, that incident changed me from being an innocent, bonded, happy young girl to a lost and lonely victim. In the unfolding days afterwards, my girlfriends turned against me, I lost my self-respect and a piece of myself. I unknowingly buried my treasure chest into a deep hole inside myself.

The hurt from these events remained always in the back of mind and I blamed myself for all that had happened. In those days there were no places for counseling and one just carried the shame and stuffed it inside, never daring to speak about it again. I didn't know all the ways it affected my life, not even understanding that I had been raped until the first time I told another person besides my then-boyfriend, Jim. That friend said to me after telling her the story, "You poor thing." Until that moment I had only blamed myself. Her comment brought a tiny place of healing as I caught a glimpse that it might not have been all my fault.

In late 1980, as Jim and I learned how to counsel, I wanted to find more healing from this trauma. With my husband's help, God showed me how the trauma had affected my relationship with my parents--because of how they had handled it. As we talked through everything over several weeks, I forgave them fully. I also saw how the friends turning against me affected my ideas about friendships. I carried fear that friends would most likely reject me. Realizing that fear made it easier to relax and enjoy people more.

The healing increased the joy of my new walk with God, cementing my understanding of my union with Him and the new ways of looking at His world. I began understanding better how to accept myself and others based on personhood rather than performance and behavior. It was easier to separate people from their behavior.

I thought the trauma was healed, but working on it just barely opened the door to uncovering my buried treasure chest. Not until almost fourteen years later, in 1994, did God bring circumstances that paralleled a bigger piece of this trauma. Those circumstances triggered a part of the buried pain that I had never realized. This time it became so big that I had to either face it or die.

The second event that greatly shaped my life was my marriage (and subsequent divorce) to Jim, the only person in those years after the rape who seemed to care and want me. We met shortly after the event and he accepted me in my shame and loved me the best he could at so young an age. Of course I clung to that acceptance in a time when everyone else was deserting me and we married very young. We both knew Jesus as our Savior and spent the next twenty years active in church, doing our best to follow God and rear our children, Jim Jr., Bob, Greg and Jodi in His ways.

We had served on CCC staff for about four years when we began learning about our freedom in Christ. The move to Atlanta in 1980 brought many changes, including another change of ministry. Through encouragement from a few friends, Jim decided that he wanted to counsel full time. We incorporated our own ministry in late 1981 and continued to live by faith for income. The years passed with many wounded people coming through the doors of Jim's office and our home. The follow-up groups in our home added fellowship and deeper Bible study for those counselees that wished to come to our home groups. Over the years, we led marriage conferences, singles' retreats and made several trips to the beach with the people in our group. They became like family and we all grew very close.

In 1993, the third event that shaped my life happened. This involved my best friend, Jenny, a vital member of our family group. I met her in 1980 shortly after moving to Atlanta. She was our first "counselee" and my best friend for thirteen years. In July of 1993, Jenny took her own life and started an avalanche that buried my treasure chest even deeper. Nothing was the same and little healing took place in the community of friends and counselees with which we were closely involved. A few of us worked together to process and heal, but the community as a whole swept it under the rug. Nothing would ever be the same again.

My heart was broken and full of questions: What caused Jenny to end her life? What did I do wrong? How could I have helped her more? What part is my fault? I cried out to God, "There is something I don't know and I want to know what it is! If I had known it, Jenny would not be dead!" We had been helping wounded people like Jenny for years and most of them were doing well. Something must be missing. By December of 1993, I had my answer. Finding that answer precipitated a crises that would stir my three big events into a huge, painful storm. The following is a brief summary about the beginning of the storm. Later I will elaborate.

That December in 1993, I went to a conference in Dallas, Texas. This handpicked, roundtable style conference allowed the participants to share what ministries they were doing that were different or unique. I shared how my husband and I had small group meetings in our home with our counselees. We had a somewhat open door policy for people to be able to talk with us whenever they needed to, which was not a common practice among many counselors.

Then two speakers shared, blasting big holes in some of my carefully studied beliefs. They were experts, from a Christian perspective, in the new field of Multiple Personality Disorder (now called Dissociative Identity Disorder) and Satanic Ritual Abuse. They also understood and believed things about the field of demonology that did not line up with my beliefs. Two messages from these experts penetrated my belief system and gave me answers to the pleas I had made to God after Jenny died. He spoke to me during these talks, bringing to my mind particular incidences with Jenny that convinced me that Christians could have demons (see *Defeating Dark Angels* by Dr. Charles Kraft for an in-depth discussion) and that MPD (DID) and Ritual Abuse were real and prevalent in our society.

At the conference, God used these messages, and then personal ministry to me, by Dr. James Wilder (JW) and Dr. Kraft to bring me relief from the trauma of losing Jenny. Dr. Kraft prayed with me and through him God brought healing for the guilt I was still carrying about her death. JW became my friend and mentor.

Even before Jenny's death, my marriage was not going well, and losing her had deepened my isolation. Because divorce was not an option, I mostly took my problems to God, but deep down I knew the marriage was not okay. Coming home from a conference with new and controversial information did not help the situation. The rift widened between my husband and me. He was not interested in what I had learned and was not happy with me for wanting to put it to use with some women I was counseling.

I knew I had to go home and tell my husband and group of friends that I had new information about MPD that might help hurting people and that I had changed my beliefs about Christians having demons. I knew this was going to be a very difficult task and I did not want to do it. It took me two weeks to tell anyone what I now believed. For the most part I got the response I had expected. Hardly anyone wanted to hear about the conference.

I finally found the courage to began talking with Jim about what I had learned. I knew it was going to be difficult and upsetting. During the conversation, I became so upset that my arms and hands were paralyzed and I could not move. I could only speak in a whisper. I had no idea what had happened until JW told me it was a physical reaction to my fear of disapproval from Jim and the fear of making a wrong decision if I followed how I felt God was leading me about the things I had learned at the conference. One of the first jewels I received concerned this fear reaction.

"The paralyzed terror you felt when you could not move and could only whisper was very sad. This is being yourself (in part) because you are seeing how frightened you are. Being ourselves is not the attractive, confident, and fun proposition we assume it will be. It does not cause us to brim with confidence, but rather it is the exposure of our true natures that allows us to no longer fear being seen. God knows full well that we are dust and that someone as messed up as we are could be in this situation. Therefore, you do not have to fear doing the wrong thing."

This jewel jolted my thinking. JW assured me that it was all right to not be all right. I could be frightened and unconfident. God already knew how bad it was anyway, and He already knew the outcome of any decision I would make. I just needed to keep listening to Him and learn better how to act like myself when in this kind of fear and pain.

There were many days of anger and hurt between Jim and me as we tried to talk, but nothing helped. My beliefs were changed and I could not go back from what I had learned. I knew it would help the women I was counseling and I could not stop trying to help them.

I clung desperately to God and to the first jewel I had received from JW at the conference--a note saying, "Of all the people here, you are doing what is the closest to what I am doing and teaching." This note from a sort of famous person gave me the courage to keep on. Nowhere in my heart could I find a place telling me to stop trying to help these women.

During the next few months I had an ongoing correspondence with JW. He gave me advice about the people with whom I was counseling and helped me learn more about the new information I had acquired at the conference. Soon the correspondence changed to questions for him about my personal life, then later to phone calls, as my life began to fall apart more and more. I told him some of my story, about being raped, about how my marriage was failing. We talked about pain and fear and how God wants to heal past wounds completely.

Misunderstandings, rejection and anger bombarded me from every direction, amplifying the pain of my failing marriage and the fact that few wanted to know what I was learning. The marriage problems spilled over into the ministry as a whole and it got so bad that I finally chose to stay away for six weeks from the meetings that were in my own home. It felt like God was the only person I had.

The stress and pain began to affect my body and I got physically ill with pneumonia. I mostly stayed in bed except to get up and go to my part time teaching job. Since I had so much time on my hands, JW sent me the manuscript for a book he was writing. I devoured it over and over. It was full of new ideas and new ways of looking at old ideas. (That book was published in 1999 as *The Red Dragon Cast Down*). Like JW says about his personal experiences shared in that book, "redemption was coming to my house" with marital conflict and emotional pain as a constant reality.

Then to complicate matters even more, God gave me a new friend that wanted to spend time with me and know me, when it seemed that no one else did. Margaret wanted to learn about my relationship with God. I felt led of God to "spiritually adopt" Margaret as I had read about in *Red Dragon Cast Down*. She would become like a daughter to me. We formed what JW called in *Red Dragon*, a love bond.

It felt so good to be loved when the pain inside was so big. Margaret's love and acceptance began thawing more of the deep, hidden pain inside. One reason for the pain inside was unknown to me--a piece that was connected to the rape. But another piece of the pain was from years of loneliness and secret hurts within my marriage. JW called the love I was receiving "rain on parched ground." In my deep distress, I clung to that love raining upon me, even though I knew it would probably worsen the marriage situation.

The "rain" continued for some weeks as the inside pain and outside conflicts escalated. Everything was falling apart. My body began paying the price of deep grief and depression. The pneumonia and depression made me wilted and barely functional. I went to stay with Margaret for the month of November 1994, trying to rest more. Just as JW had predicted, my community misunderstood that and everything else that was going on. In December I returned home for Christmas, though nothing that I did or said helped the marriage situation.

As I continued to talk with JW on the phone, I realized that God was trying to show me something more about the rape. I couldn't put my finger on it, but I wanted to see it. I did not realize how God had been setting up my situation to show me exactly that—the piece of unresolved pain from the rape.

My breaking point came in March 1995, when Margaret was unable to continue helping me. The situation was too big for her, both emotionally and physically. She basically walked out of my life. The day she left, I plunged into despair, so devastated I wanted to die. I had never hurt so badly in my life. I called my friend Debbie and asked her to come over because I was afraid of what I might do with the horrible pain. I lay on my bed with a gun in my hand, crying. From deep down inside I heard myself sob, "I just wanted her to hold me, I just wanted her to hold me!"

Instantly the Holy Spirit put His finger on that unresolved wound in my soul. "I just wanted her (my mother) to hold me! I just wanted her to hold me." Now a floodgate opened and tears gushed as I cried and cried and cried. I was so thankful that God was working this out. He had prepared me with the talks from JW. I had already committed to feel all my feelings as they came. That moment began a huge release upon which I will elaborate later.

The bond with Margaret was a wonderful blessing, but also a "set up" from God to bring deep healing, as He paralleled the past and the present. The love from Margaret paralleled the comfort I'd had from my mother all my life—until that day she found out about the rape. On that day, which Margaret's leaving again paralleled, I lost my mother as I had always known her. She was a great mom, loving, nurturing, teaching us many great things and letting us have lots of freedom to explore our world. I had grown up in a home with two loving parents in a safe and happy community. They did not know what to do with an event such as this.

When my parents learned about the rape, I know their own pain must have been tremendous. They had no resources to call upon for such a crisis. There was no place or person to turn to for counsel, so they did the best they knew. For me, that best was not good enough as days and weeks passed. As I interacted with my mother, our relationship deteriorated. I lost the comfort from a loving mother and now had to continue living with the very one who used to comfort me. I had to bury my need and longing for her comfort. Later I would understand that this was a bigger pain than the rape itself.

JW explained to me that in order to survive the tremendous pain of "losing" the loving and comforting mother that I was used to, I had to close off my need of her comfort and deny the pain of that wound. This arrested my emotional growth as a part of me closed up and died. This present crisis of feeling abandoned by friends, then losing Margaret who had been my comfort, corresponded with the crisis of the rape in the past where I also lost my mother's comfort and my friends.

A few days later I began to realize how big this pain was and how difficult it was going to be to process it along with the pain of losing ground in my marriage. My community knew how badly I had reacted to Margaret leaving. I felt even more alone and depressed as one by one people stopped talking to me. Only a few believed that I had not lost my mind, though it certainly did look like I had. All my worst fears were coming true. I had to leave home again or I might not make it.

I moved to another friend's house (Joann's) where I spent most of the next two months alone in my pain--journaling, drawing, screaming and crying out to God. During this time so alone, God showed me more about how I had not understood the depths of the wounds from the rape and how I had closed off the wound of losing my mother. Even though I had worked through some of the issues with Jim when we first learned to counsel, that bigger pain had gone unrecognized.

This poem is from my journal in 1995 when the totality of what had happened to me begin to connect to my emotions. The pain had been extremely underestimated in my heart.

The Silent Screech

I heard the screeching of my soul.
I felt the rip that tore apart.
I saw the shredded emptiness.
I knew the end before the start.

It was not a little incident
To be ignored and tossed aside.
There came an end to innocence
When those screams were held inside.

There was no place for counseling,
No understanding for repair.
Bring no more shame upon us all,
To speak again we do not dare.

For many years the scars were held,
Unknowingly their poison spread.
Outward sighs were everywhere,
I looked alive but was really dead.

The silent screech went on and on
Tearing more the delicate soul
Until there could no more contain
That ripping screech inside the hole.

Yesterday I heard the scars scream
Coming forth from inside out.
Can this be me? The horror felt?
As opened wide I heard me shout.

The rip that tore my soul that night
Destroyed all that should have been.
The life would never be the same
Until the soul was whole again.

The wound was great upon my heart.
The pain was not released or felt.
The shredded pieces lay scattered 'round
Waiting for the Master's help.

He was there and heard the cries
Buried and un-allowed that night.
He felt the pain that tore my soul
And kept me from the life and light.

He knew the darkness had to go.
He knew the rip must close and heal.
He knew the agony must come
Before His hands could love and seal.

I felt the searing pain of death.
I heard the rip, the screech from old.
I let the Master connect the times.
I let the Master take a hold.

To feel and hear the rips again
Was almost more than one could stand.
But glory came and pierced the dark
As Jesus came and held my hand.

I had to look at many things concerning this event from the past, both the first time around with my husband and now as more pain came to light. It seems that the first time around, I strongly acknowledged that the rape took place, that I was affected by my parents' handling of it and how losing my girlfriends had affected me. I had dealt with the sin in my own heart of anger and hate at how my parents handled it and I had forgiven them. I had broken an inner vow I made when my friends turned on me, ("I will never let anyone get close to me again!") and had repented of latching on to my boyfriend, Jim, instead of God. I had even looked at the meaning and consequences of being violated, how damaging it can be to take shame and blame, and how it hurt not being listened to, not being heard. But I had not known that I buried the pain of losing my mother while having to continue living with her. I had not *felt* that buried pain and feeling it was necessary for healing.

In my loneliness with only God and my journal, I went back over every aspect I could think of concerning that time in my youth. I wanted it all clean and healed. Over a period of weeks, I faced and felt the pain of being left deeply wounded with a dead place in my soul. I examined my heart for any other sins, for feelings of self-hatred, for feelings that no one was there for me. My buried treasure chest came slowly back into the light.

Jewels from JW during this time were numerous. In one phone conversation he asked me to tell him about my trauma. As I did so, I felt extremely loved and calmed that someone really cared. He said, *"The people around you tried to do some good things, but they failed."* JW said this with such love and compassion that even failure began having a new meaning for me. The lack of condemnation in his voice for those who had failed me helped me see the situation with compassion for everyone involved. Knowing God's love for me, and the work I had done earlier with Jim, had already cleansed much of the negative, but JW's kindness made failure less harsh. He reminded me, "To try and then most likely fail is about all we humans can do."

As we talked on the phone, JW pointed out that a process of spiritual death was now in motion. It reminded me of the words Jesus said about a "grain of wheat must fall into the earth and die" so that it can become something new. Things in my life were going to be changed so drastically that the results would look and feel like a death had definitely taken place. Much of my way of life would be different and new.

"Now the present crisis has set you up for a collision course with dying to the issues this trauma created in your life. You are additionally going through 4 or 5 other deaths concurrently [relationships with friends, marriage, belief systems in my heart]. When you die, take all areas of your life. Get the other areas lined up, too. You will die and you won't be the same person. All your relationships will die and at the end you will be different. Pull as many parts in as you can. The new person will have all the parts together. Only if you try to fight it will you kill yourself. This is not something to do in your own strength. You will wish you were dead, but don't fight the pain. Few will want to be with you because most people cannot stand to be there when someone is dying or dead. All the details are in God's hands. Any love bonds you have will survive because love is not affected by death. Fear will be affected by death. Many remaining fears will blow away. Yes, you went through this process before in 1980 [when I learned who I was in Christ and my husband and I worked on the trauma] and connected that pain to part of the trauma, forgiving the things you knew about then, but this is a different part of it. You did not know the depths of the wounds and how you had closed up so tightly inside."

The phone conversations continued weekly as JW helped me bring all the new thoughts and understandings together, in order to face how long I had hurt and how deeply I had covered up the pain of my rape, as well as the pain in my marriage. Because I couldn't admit how needy I was to my mother after the rape, I had turned to Jim for security and formed what JW calls a trauma bond with him. A trauma bond is one that is formed during intensity and neediness and is not healthy like a love bond. It was part of what had to die. Only God would know the outcome of the death and what would be resurrected. As I walked through the new insights, JW continually encouraged me to say over and over, *even if unheeded*, "I hurt, I am very,

very needy. This is who I am right now. I need help." That was very difficult to do because few seemed to even want to hear or help me. But it was necessary in order to get in touch with those old buried feelings.

These are the three events that most shaped my life. God continued to work deeply for the next few years bringing me through this part of my journey. Although I, like all Christians, am a jewel in the making, I like to call what JW told me during these years "Jewels," because I treasured every word that I heard over the phone as they opened my eyes of understanding to new ways of walking with God. And they were like pearls of wisdom spoken of in the Scriptures.

Now that I have given an overview of the three events that greatly affected my life, I will share topics that I discussed with JW (Dr. Wilder), either by letter or by phone. As the brewing storm grew to engulf almost every area of my life, I struggled daily to make sense of the destruction. God was my anchor, along with JW who was my human lifeline.

Even as I clung to God, questions tore at my heart. "Where is God in all this mess?" "Where is the faith on which I've stood for so many years?" "How do some issues like submission, co-dependency, Godly suffering, explaining myself, priorities, fit into what is happening in my life?" "Did I ever know anything I thought I knew?" "Should I stop helping the ladies that I'm counseling?" "How much more pain and conflict can I stand?"

The questions were strong and unanswerable. "What will happen to our ministry organization?" "How will we live financially if people stop supporting us?" "Our children are going to suffer." "What am I causing, Lord?"

These are only a few of the questions that constantly crisscrossed my mind. I didn't think I would live through the storm as it billowed and darkened.

ON ANGER

Much of the darkness I'd experienced through the years in my marriage came from the way my husband handled his anger. There never seemed to be any lasting changes, though I had occasionally talked to a counselor about the hurt it brought me. Believing that divorce was not an option drove me to

God. I asked Him to do whatever He needed to in me to help the situation. I truly wanted to love and accept Jim as he was.

At various stages through the years, I begged and pleaded with Jim to find out what was going on with him. I seldom responded well to any rage coming my way and usually felt that I somehow deserved it. Over and over I went back to God, pleading for Him to change me so I could accept or prevent the anger coming my way. Bit by bit it wore me down until this period in my life where I could hardly function. I no longer had an anchor to hold my sanity and know what to believe about myself. Was I truly crazy about this whole situation? As a told JW how bad I felt and talked with him about finding my way he responded at different times with these jewels:

"Nothing justifies taking out feelings on another. Nothing justifies taking out feelings on another."

In a letter, JW actually wrote this statement twice about the struggle I was having over how Jim handled anger. My debate did not exactly have words but it felt something like this: *What is wrong with me that he is angry with me so much? Is this anger displaced or do I deserve it? I have done everything I know from my perspective and power to fix us. I can't take this anymore.* JW helped me look at my struggle differently. Even if I did something to bring anger from another, it was not all right to take those feelings out on me. Harmful anger was not okay at all.

In my co-dependent thinking, I felt I deserved the rage that came at me. From my view, sometimes the anger I received was just from doing something that was like me to do. Maybe it was just irritating and not really a sin, but I seldom distinguished between the two. I just took the rage as deserved and begged God to change me so I wouldn't do the irritating things anymore. Slowly but surely over many years, I lost myself as I tried to become different enough to prevent the anger. It was not working.

"Anger represents to you an attack on your very identity. It destroys the deepest part of you."

JW assured me that I was not crazy to be upset and hurt by my perception of Jim's problem. He said words that I had never heard before. In the past, two different times that I had asked someone for help, both of them had told me in so many words, "Your husband's anger is your fault and if you will just change, he won't be angry with you any more." These words were from people in authority whom I trusted. These words set me on the

scribed above. Now for the first time, I heard something
t.

have a relationship with a defense mechanism, only with a person. Anger is a defense mechanism. Denial is a defense mechanism. Beliefs and feelings can be defense mechanisms. Showering someone with gifts, etc, can be a defense. It is not possible to relate with someone when they are hiding behind defenses. The road out for the defender is to see that nothing works, despair of it ever working and see what is really in the heart come out."

JW assured me that I could feel angry and "not sin."

"If I act like myself when angry there will be healing instead of power words, because who I am is a loving, bonding person."

Further comments helped me see anger differently:

"Anger is the fear of being hurt. Rejection is the fear of abandonment."

* Page 124 *The Red Dragon*

"You need to know how you want to respond to anger and rejection. They will always be around."

"Anger and rejection are misguided calls for closeness."

"In an abusive environment you are never to make the abuser feel bad. If you act wounded they will get furious."

"An abuser feels powerless so he or she abuses. He does not see that he has *some* power because he *is* having an effect on something. He goes by his feelings."

Although JW's words were helpful to ponder, it took many months of practice and more healing before I could live free from fear of anger.

ON SUBMISSION

Shortly after returning home from the conference in 1993, one of the first topics that I discussed with JW concerned one of these big questions I had. What about the issue of submission? It was a topic that I had studied, taught and applied to my own life, but I was having a difficult time reconciling what God had shown me there at the conference and the fact that Jim disapproved about how I had changed. What was I to do? It felt at first like I had to choose between God and Jim. I began to realize that my fear of disapproval from my husband was allowing him to be my god, something neither of us wanted. The words that JW sent me in a letter helped clear the problem for me. He approached the subject of submission a little differently than I had heard before. This is the letter he sent January 8, 1994:

> You mentioned that you were thinking again about submission. When the Bible speaks of submission it uses the Greek word *hupotasso. Hupotasso* is made up of *hupo*, which is a prefix meaning from, of or under; and the more difficult to define *tasso*. *Tasso* means ordained, appointed or addicted. This suggests a meaning for the word *hupotasso* as under appointment. Most interest in the meaning of *hupotasso* is generated by its use in the commands to *hupotasso* either husbands or government. It is often confused with the word obey (*Hupakouo* 5219) but *hupotasso* means something different than obey. (Obey=*Hupakouo*: Mark 1:27, 4:41, Luke 8:25, 17:6, Acts 6:7, 12:13, Romans 6:12, 16, 17, 10:16, Ephesians 6:1, 5, Philippians 2:12, Colossians 3:20, 22, 2 Thessalonians 1:8, 3:14, Hebrews 5:9, 11:8, 1 Peter 3:6.
>
> *Hupotasso* on the other hand when used as a description always means doing what God wants, often in direct opposition to what the being involved wants. (Cf: Luke 10:17.)
>
> Second in the writings of St. Paul, where we most often encounter the word, there is an overwhelming push for unity of all believers in doing what God wants. The message of Ephesians is that if we realized that we were one body, conflict and sin

would end as we all did what God wants. It is possible that for Paul *hupotasso* means almost the same as *Agape* (love). (CF: 1 Corinthians 13.) This does not seem likely to me since we are also instructed to *hupotasso* governments, which clearly does not mean to love government.

At this point St. Peter is the most helpful, both by example and explanation. Peter is not talking about the perfect Christ-like ideal, as Paul does. Peter is concerned with real life. His instruction to servants to *hupotasso* their masters is followed by the interesting observation that the servant may be beaten for so doing. This obviously means that the master may very well not like the *hupotasso* from a servant! But the servant receives praise from God for <u>doing what is right</u>. This suggests that *hupotasso* means <u>being under commission from God to do what is right for the other person, whether they want it or like it or not.</u>

Peter also gives us an example of *hupotasso* to government on several occasions. First he states to the religious authorities in Acts that, "we must obey God rather than men." Thus he gives an example of *hupotasso* to church authorities, as did Stephen (an example to Paul). Peter was also the first Christian "jail breaker." He was escorted out of jail by an angel, clearly against the laws of the day and against the wishes of the authorities. This example of *hupotasso* to government again underlines the meaning of doing what is right in God's eyes regardless of whether the other party likes it or not. This jailbreak also cost the lives of several guards who were punished for letting him escape. This implies that we are not to make the decision based on the consequences to others or to ourselves—as in John the Baptist's *hupotasso* when he condemned Herod, and as a result was beheaded. *Hupotasso* is solely on the basis of what is right to God.

There is an implied teaching about *hupotasso* in the case of Annannias and Saphira. Here the husband dies for telling a lie to the church and hours later his wife agrees with him--as opposed to doing what is right. If the *hupotasso* meant obey your husband and doing what he wanted, then she should have been in *hupotasso,* but instead she died on the spot for her lack of doing what God said was right whether her husband liked it or not.

With these examples, it should be clear that *hupotasso* cannot mean to obey, to please, to do what people want, or to make someone happy. The context would define *hupotasso* as "doing what is right in God's eyes in regard to a situation or person—whether they like it or not, and regardless of the consequences to you or others for so doing." Study the passages for yourself and see if you agree.

Hupotasso:

Used in descriptions. Usually non volitional or against the will

To Spirits--Luke 10:17, 20

To God or His Laws—Romans 8:7, 20 10:3, 1 Corinthians 15:27, 28, Ephesians 1:22, Philippians 3:21, Hebrews 2:5, 8; 12:9, 1 Peter 3:22

To People--Luke 2:51, 1 Corinthians 14:32, 1 Peter 3:5

Used in instructions. All volitional

To Government--Romans 13:1, 5 Titus 3:1, 1 Peter 2:13

To Church --1 Corinthians 14:32, 34 16:16, Ephesians 5:21, 1 Peter 5:5

To Masters—Titus 2:9 1Peter 2:18

To Husbands—Ephesians 5:22-24 Colossians 3:18, Titus 2:5 1 Peter 3:1, 5

To God—James 4:7

Well, this is probably more than you wanted from your comment about submission but I hope you find something here to uplift you.

In Christ, Jim Wilder

These jewels helped me with the struggle I was having. The issue was more about doing what God says and what is right for the other person, even if my consequences were unpleasant. In following God no matter how it looked and felt to others, I would be doing what was right for everyone, even if I received disapproval, and even if they did not like what I was doing. Because I craved approval so much, this was not going to be easy to walk out.

ON CO-DEPENDENCY

Along with questions about submission, I asked JW about codependency. It was a popular topic and I wanted to know his views. At times I was unable to distinguish *agape love* (God's kind of love) from codependent love. Most of my life I had been very giving and serving. But was it love or was it unhealthy? These two topics, submission and co dependency, whirled around in my thinking until I was lost in what the truth really was.

"The best way I know to judge between a*gape* love and co-dependency concerns my attitude about the outcome. If I act in order to obtain an outcome, I'm codependent. If I act because my character or spirit impels me, even though it won't work or might not work, it is a*gape.* A*gape* is not related to success or probable response, it is dependent only on the character of the one acting."

I continually returned to these topics for the next few years as God took me through the differences. I knew I was often guilty of trying to fix things and keep peace. I also knew that much of my life had been lived as a*gape.* I wanted to be clear on the differences, to live from my heart and not take condemnation when it was not there.

"Mature people set others free, but keep the relationship intact."

"Co-dependency is trying to save the other from their pain, fix, enable, or remove their pain. A*gape* love sits with them in it or uses 'tough love.'"

Little did I know until after this early letter how gu
interfering with Jim feeling his own pain.

"Taking away suffering that belongs to someone e
love, if it keeps that person from learning from his or h
When pain is shared it teaches that when necessary, pai
endured." * Paraphrased from *The Red Dragon, p. 176*

God began showing me as I talked with JW how often I related co-dependently in my marriage. It was a big eye opener to understand that I been feeling my husband's feelings instead of letting him feel them. I had to stop doing this. I often deferred to his anger and verbal abuse when I should have stood up against it, knowing that a boundary had been crossed. I saw that my strength was the sand upon which much of our life had been built. JW said it was good sand, but sand still the same. The whirlwind in my mind grew worse as I added the question of Godly suffering and justifying to the mix of submission and codependency. Underlying fears surfaced so that I could no longer deny them. I was a mess and could not find an anchor anymore. I could barely help myself, much less any one else who felt anxious around me. JW reassured me:

"If someone else falls apart right now, you do not have to recover to fix it. You can't fix it. You are not supposed to."

"It is not up to you to manage anyone else's anxiety or feelings."

"You must get to the place where you will recognize by your radar that a boundary has been stepped on."

"All of your love for others has not been co-dependent or rescuing. You truly are a loving person."

ELING HURT AND HARM

hers' feelings for them and I was
boundary, I asked JW, "How do I
ffering or experiencing pain that
tian-wife teeth on the passage in
such a way as to win their
els about the difference in

mething Godly that we desire to do. For
your child required you to suffer in some way, wild
es could not keep you from doing it."

"When we are being beaten up, we want to get out of there. God can redeem this kind of evil, but it is still not the same—it is an evil thing to hurt someone. Test it internally—if wild horses cannot keep you from doing it, then it is Godly and Biblical suffering. Allowing yourself to be harmed is not Biblical suffering."

"Godly suffering endures hardship so others might know who they are." **The Red Dragon, p. 286*

"When you want to get away from hurt—go. If you're diving under water, holding your breath, eventually you want to get a breath. This does not mean you won't ever dive again."

"When your big desire is to be like Christ, 'Your suffering is His glory.'" (Philippians 3: 10)

ON LOVE BONDS

The mess I was in did not deter me from loving and helping the women to whom I was ministering. By now I had spiritually adopted two women (more on that later) and there was much love among us. One of the most important things that JW did for me in the beginning of our relationship was to tell me how he and God see me. He told me that I was a "loving, bonding, nurturing person." The work I was doing with these women was proof of that. Hearing that I was a loving, bonding and nurturing person was one thing. It was another to believe it. For years I had been hearing the opposite from my husband and a few other people I loved and trusted. If one can ever be justified in calling names, looking at some of my actions would have done it, but as a child and young person I had been loving and nurturing. It began to dawn on me that over the years I had become more like those names and not like what I had been as a child. JW's words went deeply into my soul. I held on to them and wanted to know that they were true.

As I slowly realized that I had come to believe and thus live out much of the negative with which others had labeled me, and because of these labels and the unfinished trauma pain, over the years I had unknowingly lost myself. I agreed with the false labels. What I had learned about my identity in Christ had partially changed my self-perception, but what I was hearing from JW caused me to look deeper. In spite of knowing my identity in Christ, I had not broken completely free of how others evaluated me. Many of those evaluations were not my true characteristics at all.

As I meditated on JW's evaluation that I am loving, bonding and nurturing, *The Red Dragon* manuscript gave me new words for relating and connecting to others (and myself). JW called them bonds—love bonds, fear bonds, trauma bonds. He gave me many jewels about bonds, using examples in my own life to illustrate them. The first is my favorite. I couldn't believe what he was saying:

"You are a loving, bonding, nurturing person who wants love bonds not fear bonds."

A strong love bond allows negative and positive feelings but does not want the bond to be broken."

"The strongest bonds are the ones that will work any time day or night, no matter how intense or bad things get." * *The Red Dragon, p. 321*

"Bonding stirs people up to the core. You must define your bond and not let any others in the community around you deter you with their own fears."

"Our goal in love is to have openness to all people simultaneously."

"People have to feel loved enough to express deep grief."

"We fear our emotional needs will bring rejection so we hide them. Truth must be held in love bonds—'you can be part of a family that never ends and that bond can start with me.'" * *The Red Dragon, p. 321*

"The closer we get to someone, the more God shows us what is in our heart."

I continued to cling to any encouraging words from JW. In a letter I received in May 1994, JW encouraged me to keep going, even in the face of opposition from those around me. The other woman that I had spiritually adopted was living in our home. Sometimes we had conflicts. I related some of these incidents to JW. Again, his words went very deep, were so contrary to most of the messages I'd been receiving:

"There is so much I wish to learn from your spirit. The courage and boldness to love that is inside you is an inspiration to me. When you wrote of your joy in kissing goodnight the grumpy face of one of your 'spiritually adopted daughters,' it reminds me so of my own 'daughter' that I must laugh. You must be nearly impossible to live with and yet so irresistible. It makes me think of Jesus' words to Simon the Pharisee about the woman in his house, 'Her great love shows that she has been forgiven much.' The sweetness of such love is such that it seems almost sacrilegious to receive, as though we were taking something so delicate that it belongs to God alone, yet we must receive it or it will be destroyed. How much like the water that David's mighty men brought back from the well this love is, and we need only kiss grumpy faces and share some grief. How blessed you are."

ON PAIN (Letter June 20, 1994)

I received a letter from JW with an article he had written specifically about helping men learn to feel their pain. This is one of the jewels that he does not advise using with a young Christian or a person with Child or Infant maturity. Seek God's wisdom before taking this as a way to help yourself or another. JW sent the letter to encourage me that this would help my husband if he would look at it. Instead it helped me, as it may other women. These ideas were paramount in helping me stop feeling another person's feelings for them as well as teaching me to feel my own pain.

"Thank you for your recent letter. I was touched that you would share your struggle with me. I am enclosing an excerpt from something I am writing that I call Pain Lab. Men have learned from childhood how to avoid emotional pain and keep themselves out of discomfort by getting angry with people who trigger these feelings. As someone once told me, "It is easier to control you than to control my feelings." Our part then is to become very difficult to control and let our loved ones have their feelings. Pain Lab is a process when men stop avoiding painful feelings by escaping them or controlling others, and begin to learn how to feel terrible and still carry on. It is the benefit of boot camp in the military to teach recruits that there is something more important than avoiding pain. Pain Lab is usually forced on men but a wise man will choose it for himself.

Pain Lab Requirements:

A six months' period of time, in which you actively disable all your mechanisms for avoiding uncomfortable situations and feelings. This would include but not be limited to the following:

No drugs, alcohol, masturbation, sexually explicit materials.

No withdrawing, lying, extended work hours, or use of recreation to avoid conflicts.

No controlling others through threats, anger or other intense emotions.

The first two weeks are devoted to observing all types of ways in which you avoid emotional pain.

Week two through the end of the third month is devoted to actively resisting all known and newly found ways to avoid painful emotions and fear. The objective is to locate and feel as intensely as possible all discomforting emotions.

To do this, one must focus on each emotion as it appears and feel it as strongly as possible until it disappears on its own. This should be done a minimum of 10 times per day and up to 200 times a day on weekends or times of strong feelings.

During this time it is also important to increase the amount of input you receive by being truthful to others about the things you normally hide from them for your own comfort. This exercise should be guided by two principles. One: you must say the things you fear to say. Two: the objective is to feel your own feelings, not to upset others and make them feel your feelings for you.

The last three months of the six are devoted to a continuation of the painful feelings but by now there should be considerably less time spent trying to avoid pain and an increasing ability and pride in the ability to feel your own feelings. If you are still trying hard to avoid feelings (or avoiding them without much effort) by the end of the fourth month you will require professional help in overcoming your avoidance.

The objective overall is to remove fear-based actions and reactions that result in avoidance, concealing, threatening and controlling and to replace them with desire-based behavior. By the end of six months you should be doing things that are deeply meaningful to you even when they require feeling unpleasant feelings. Your relationships should be characterized by pursuing the desirable, not avoiding the unpleasant.

This process is difficult to achieve and sustain. Most men do not stay with it without the encouragement and participation of other men. You are free to try on your own and risk a high probability of failure or seek the comfort of other men who are similarly facing pain.

Barbara, this is a bit of what I would be thinking in your situation.
Love, Jim"

I took three things from this article as being for me personally: I would have to become very hard to control by not allowing another's feelings or opinion about me to sway me. I would have to learn how to stop feeling other people's feelings for them so they would have to feel them for themselves, not fixing their feelings or allowing myself to be manipulated into a place where I would take the upset onto myself. I would begin practicing feeling every feeling until it stopped. (More on that later)

As I began to put some of this into practice and allow others' to feel their own feelings instead of me feeling them, JW told me that in doing this, my actions (or lack thereof) would likely be misconstrued. It would look unfeeling and unloving.

"You must keep clearly in mind what you want the outcome to be and not let anyone talk you into agreeing on something less. You must not agree with accusations even out of frustration. You must not give in to fear."

These things were very difficult to do and it took a long time to get them through my head. Little did I know that God was getting ready to work some more on the effects of my trauma at fourteen.

Feeling every feeling until it stops was a very new concept to me. I think that of all the things that JW taught me, how to look differently at emotional pain stands out as one of the most valuable jewels. I learned about pain in three ways—how to feel my own, what to do with others' pain, and how evil people use pain. I will separate the jewels on pain into these three categories. **First** what pain means to us personally.

"Feel as bad as you need to feel. This is the road to freedom."

"Pain lab seems to be the correction for those who fear pain and are therefore slaves to avoiding pain. Running from pain makes us Dragon fodder." [The Red Dragon is JW's nickname for Satan.]

"If you can't cry, you are short on comfort."

"Tell the truth about pain—it hurts."

"It is very painful to you when someone withdraws their love—even if it is just to take their hand from you when they disagree or are hurt by something you said. It takes great love not to withdraw and shut someone out even when you are hurt."

This was one of the things that I wanted God to make very real in my own life. It has become so clear to me when someone I love does this. I try to address this issue immediately when it arises, so that there is more chance to keep the intimacy. I do not want to do it to anyone else.

"We can return to joy only from the misery we confess." ** The Red Dragon, p. 125*

"When you can't think straight, stop thinking and feel."

"You can't make pain manageable by talking about it. Pain is not manageable."

"It takes great courage to hold on to God during times of great hurt."

"There are many ways to process pain," said JW. "Scream, (Isaiah 58:1 says, 'Cry loudly, do not hold back; raise your voice like a trumpet...') It releases energy and is a useful stress reliever. Draw your screams. Use colors, pictures, write words. Advertise that you are not okay. Let it be okay to struggle, to feel bothered, to be confused. Stay there as long as you feel and need to. You've been keeping yourself okay in order to insulate others; you feel their feelings for them because if they get depressed it will scare you. Let others feel their own feelings. Feel whatever. It may not be true, but it won't destroy you."

"Get a cycle going of HURT- CRY-COMFORT-PLAY. Move around. Do things that satisfy you. Find out what is satisfying. Ride a bike, play jacks. Play. 'Good kids' sit still, but they are not acting like themselves."

"The power of love comes from its ability to suffer pain it does not deserve. When we suffer, we are the source of good things. We are good to be around because love flows from us."

"When pain and damage are here it brings joy. Embrace it because you know you are due for a healing and will be shown a mystery."

"Your identity is based on Christ. It is one based on love—a love so solid it can endure all pain. God is certain that if we know Him, we will love Him. The Dragon wants our identities to be based on fear. He doesn't expect to be loved. He knows we FEAR PAIN."

"Bring your pain to Jesus and see what it means. Don't hide your pain or you won't see what Heaven sees and be healed. It helps to have someone with you. A loving relationship is necessary for the trip to Heaven."

"If you discount the pain, you will reduce the redemption value, too."

Many tried to hurry me through my pain, calling it various things, rejecting me because I did not look like I was "spiritual" and trusting God. It was pulling on their fears and they wanted me to get over it. This is a poem I wrote in my journal about the hurrying:

Lord Of the Sabbath (Matthew 12:3-8, Mark 7:1-8)

You stumped the Pharisees of old
You wouldn't keep the rules they made.
You healed upon the Sabbath day
To eat you crushed the heads of grain.

Today there are still Pharisees
They're everywhere within Your Church.
They see not the person's agony
Nor feel their awful pain and hurt.

Unto their own invented rules
They cling and hold so hard and tight.
Afraid to loosen hold the grip
No way to flow the love and light.

Pain must not show to Pharisees
Don't upset traditions held.
The elders do not want to see
The precious ways and systems failed.

The rules were made Your agenda to serve
Not made to keep us tutored long.

Mercy not sacrifice is what you want
Love is now Your agenda strong.

The Pharisees all hope it's quick
The fixes that You bring to me.
Don't mess us up with pain and tears
Your hurts must hurry so we don't see.

The Pharisees are hard to please
They want to show some easy ways.
Weary and tired of helping some
They hurry or reject my days.

Some Pharisees Your people are
Honoring with their lips and hearts.
But do not want to hear new pain
Instead they judge my hurting parts.

Lord of the Sabbath is who You are
The needs of people are allowed.
It matters not which day they come
As long as they're helpless and yielded, bowed.

Oh, Son of Man, my Lord You are
Fill me with the love You sent.
I never want again to be
One who condemns the innocent.

In Gethsemane I know You were
These last months I was there, too.
There is no rule for curing pain
The only answer's to feel it with You.

Committing to feel all my feelings until they stopped meant that I was not going to hurry.

The **second** thing I learned about pain involved JW's statement--*Pain means comfort is on the way.* I've not found anyone yet who already knew this. Avoiding pain at all costs is the common thinking about pain. That is because very few people have been comforted in their pain. Even if they were comforted as a child, they learned somewhere to turn away from the one causing the pain. But God intended pain to mean *comfort is on the way*. Even in child rearing, if it is done correctly, the child will not run away from the one who hurt them. (This means everyday hurts, not abuse, though many abused children continue to go back to an abusive parent, hoping it will change.) Children will continue to seek comfort even from a love- bonded parent who hurts them. Comfort can come in many forms—listening, safe touches, holding, a few words when wanted. These jewels helped me know about comforting others in their pain.

"The message is to be, 'I am glad to be with you even while you are in pain.' When we have learned that pain is not to be avoided, we can hurt with someone even though we don't enjoy the pain."

"When you hurt with someone else in their pain, even though you don't enjoy it, eventually it will help you validate your own pain, that it really did hurt and you needed someone to hurt with you. No one shared your pain. All this will bring healing to you."

"Children who are not taught otherwise think pain means they have no value. If they were important, someone would protect them. But pain reflects how valuable we are in the face of evil. Paul told the Philippians that his suffering was their glory and told the Colossians that it was his joy to suffer. (Philippians 2:17, Colossians 1:24) * *The Red Dragon, p. 286*

"Hurting with someone shows their great value"

"A good parent will teach her child how to understand pain and endure or remember things without fear."

"No one has to fix anyone's pain; we just need to sit with them in it. It cannot be fixed, only healed.""

"Share pain. This is a sign that the person is of great value that we are willing to suffer with them so they do not have to suffer alone. This teaches them they do not need to fear pain."

" Giving safe affection is a way to comfort that meets many needs at once. It says, 'You are worth keeping safe.'"

"Pain is the single largest reason we do not mature. When the community does not provide what we need, we hurt. When we fear hurting, we stop maturing until redemption appears to get us through." * *The Red Dragon, p. 285*

"Pain is an invitation to draw close and heal. It is lifted when shared by another. It says 'you are of great value, it can be endured and it will be lifted'".

"People revert to skills learned as a baby when they feel insecure. They are desperate to avoid fear and pain if they were not comforted then, and they turn to the other coping skills." * *The Red Dragon, p. 81*

The **third** thing that JW taught me about pain was how evil uses it. We get these three categories of pain all confused and intertwined by the wiles of the enemy. From *The Stages of A Man's Life,* I paraphrase:

> "When a person avoids pain it means that his or her pain must be borne by someone else. Perhaps this is a good definition of evil—'the result of making others bear our pain.' These people try to take control, because if they are in control they don't have to feel pain. Two favorite ways to avoid pain by taking control are threats and blaming. Although Jesus experienced extreme pain, He never threatened or blamed. (1 Peter 2:23)
>
> When we try to control something that cannot be controlled, it will make us feel out of control. We really cannot control anyone. We can hope to influence in a positive way, but we cannot control. Even God's two children (Adam and Eve) blew it because He did not control them. When things went wrong, God did not ask whose fault it was, He only wanted to know, 'What happened here?' Feeling or being made to feel another's pain is not a picture of Biblical pain bearing (suffering)." ***The Stages of a Man's Life, pp.* 53 and 54

"Pain is the easiest way for evil to produce fear. More pain means more fear, which means more power over others—<u>except for those who do not fear pain.</u> This is why we must learn not to fear pain."

I wasn't certain what JW meant by "Those who don't fear pain." He explained that when one endures suffering as a faithful servant, the fear of pain goes away. "Satanists fear pain but they don't fear using it on others. We who have suffered are free from the fear itself."

ON GRIEF AND LOSS

The storm clouds darkened as time passed. My body began paying the toll for the emotional tempest inside. JW explained why the pain was so big and how important it was to grieve.

"Your letter says that you are 'wilted, depressed, almost lost the will to live, empty, useless, wouldn't say, 'I would choose life.' It seems you are in a significant depression. The acceptance you are receiving from the love bond with Margaret is pointing up the extent of your rejection and loss throughout life. You are grieving and it would be good to focus some attention on that."

"When old feelings from lacks in our lives begin to be acknowledged, especially by someone who loves us, the pain from the lack of love thaws and the feelings get very intense. The feelings you have been and are avoiding are 'Nobody wants me, especially when I am upset.' It is intolerable to be ignored when upset. You are going to have to feel how much it hurts when 'nobody wants me'. You learned after your trauma that if you are needy, you are bad. If you have to feel how much it hurts when nobody wants you, how will you do it and express it? Because of the love bond with Margaret, you almost have enough courage to feel how awful it feels.

You are in transition (labor) and you could give birth to 'Nobody wants me.' (My God, my God, why have you forsaken me?). You need someone steady enough to say, 'I'll be here and let you feel this, I don't want you'—and in the peak you will feel they don't either. If they try to fix it, then you can't birth it. Rather than leaving the message, 'I'm not ok' to chance-- advertise—'I am in the biggest trouble I've ever been in. I may lose my sanity.'"

Speaking of the love, nurture and comfort I had been giving to the ladies I was ministering to, not leaving them when misunderstandings bombarded me, JW assured me that I was on the right track:

"Unless we give what we never received we will not grieve deeply. You gave to others in their great pain, not abandoning or deserting them. Now you will grieve deeply that you did not have that comfort in the past nor do you have quite enough now."

"When you have poured out your life, done your best, want it to turn out right and it doesn't—for even an hour—grieve. Feel the grief and sadness. If you have thoughts like, 'I'm bad' or 'It's my fault'-- it is time to grieve. Worry is an *avoidance* of grief that something can't turn out okay. It is avoiding feeling sad."

"Most families communicate to children as they are growing up and get upset, 'Now, now,' or 'Don't cry,' with the end result that most of us learn, 'No one wants to be with me when I am upset.'"

"Just grieving does not redeem (make something good out of the mess) our story—seeing through the eyes of Heaven does."

"If we try to redeem our own suffering we settle for less than if we had embraced the suffering. Redemption is God's work."

"You have layers and layers of losses—an enormous stack. Are you getting a picture of the size of the truck that ran over you?"

Slowly, I was getting the picture.

ON SPIRITUAL ADOPTION

Although I'd had ample warning reading the *Red Dragon* manuscript, I was not prepared for how controversial JW's jewels on Spiritual adoption would be. Isn't it strange how we read something and think, "Well, that won't be the way it is in my life." It was.

Just as Jenny had become part of our family before she died, Margaret and a few others were quickly growing just as close to Jim and me. Being friends while counseling someone at the same time involves almost daily contact. I used to call this kind of relationship "re-parenting." When I met JW, he called it "Spiritual adoption." He was quick to say that it is something that God has to do and cannot be taken lightly. I loved having these close relationships, but my community did not understand and later they even began to contribute to the marital conflict. Thunder pealed from the clouds.

"Expect rejection, misunderstanding, criticism, doubt, suspicion, hostility, and distancing from other people, especially when things get worse and you could really use some help, understanding and support." * *The Red Dragon, p. 323* People are often afraid of what they don't understand.

"You are still a mother even if no one appreciates it. Children do not make one a mother- they only provide the opportunity to express it. For mothers, satisfaction is found by bringing out the best in themselves and their children and giving without receiving in return."

"Success in Spiritual adoption is not based on outcome. Love will not heal most damage and healing may not remove it." * *The Red Dragon, p. 321*

Spiritual adoption is not only for the adopted one, but also for the adopter. God doesn't work in a vacuum. JW told me that adoption would bring out gaps in my own development (maturity stages) and I would get healing. Little did I know that while I was enjoying the "rain on parched ground" from Margaret, that God was about to turn my world upside down.

Adoption will bring out the gaps in your own development and you will find healing for yourself.

Let the adoptee know your weaknesses. We are not able to give life and we will fail them, so do not hide weaknesses. Only God can give life.

When a wounded, traumatized person is adopted, the love they receive can bring up the pain that they have kept at bay. Instead of getting "better" they may get "worse" at first. JW explained it like this:

"When trauma arises from the absence of necessary love and care, this produces feelings of abandonment, rejection, despair, loneliness, loss, depression and grief. These feelings remain frozen inside the child/adult and thaw in the presence of love. Comfort, care and love bring out the pain very quickly. New spiritual parents commonly assume that more love will make the pain go away. Instead it thaws more pain, increasing the feelings. Immature people may break the bonds at this point. It's very important to admit failures, but do not break bonds." *Paraphrased from page 321, *The Red Dragon.*

The concept of thawing pain would soon become easy for me to understand, because that was exactly what Margaret's love was going to do for me—make me realize what I had lost. When she broke the bond a few weeks later, the pain was almost unbearable. JW assured me that I was not crazy to feel so hurt. Both of the losses, my mother and Margaret were very real and painful.

"When you have a genuine bond and it gets torn apart, there will be extreme pain. Suppose you have a baby about 6 months old and you can't see it for several weeks. Would you be sipping lemonade? NO! You would be hysterical."

Spiritually adopting Margaret did not turn out the way I thought it would in the end, but I do not regret going through it. In some ways we both benefited greatly. There is no way for a human being to make things work out. As JW told me,

"Even when a Spiritual adoption is ordained by God, we cannot make it work. 'Unless the Lord builds the house, they labor in vain who build it.'" (Psalm 127:1).

"The goal is not so much for them to get well as it is to fill their joy bucket and help them live life."

(For a more extensive discussion of Spiritual adoption, see *The Red Dragon Cast Down*, Guidelines for Spiritual Bonding, pp. 320-324, or *Life Model* by JW)

ON CLARIFYING AND EXPLAINING VS JUSTIFYING AND DEFENDING

As the marriage conflicts continued to worsen, the misunderstandings got stormier. Trying to communicate under this kind of stress is almost impossible. When Jim and I tried to discuss our differences, I would not feel in my heart that I was defensive, though accused of it. I did not have a clear understanding of how to explain myself when the other person wouldn't listen. JW helped clear the difference between clarifying myself and being defensive:

"Explaining yourself is a tricky area because while we do not need to justify ourselves, from age 4 up we do need to clarify ourselves. We have half the responsibility of making our communication understandable to others. I find I must constantly explain to others who I am or they will take me for someone I am not. Yet I can do no better than offer others the opportunity to understand me—the rest is up to them and it is hard work.... The difference between explaining and justifying oneself is one of focus.

With justifying, the focus is on whether the hearer's feelings are assuaged, 'can I change their mind,' while explaining oneself is focused on personal satisfaction-- have I said what I need to say? That is to say, 'when I am pleased that I have expressed what I wanted to say,' I can stop. Rather than thinking, 'when you are pleased by my explanation I can stop.'"

I still hold to this jewel today because it is still difficult for me to be misunderstood. I check my motive and remind myself that it is okay to clarify.

ON COMING AND GOING

As God opened my eyes to the unhealthy ways I related to my husband, what JW told me about coming and going was the most shocking jewel I'd heard so far. We talked about that topic more than once. It was foreign to my thinking. This jewel is another that takes careful and prayerful consideration. It is not to be taken lightly or as an excuse for separating from or leaving a marriage. It is a principle to be honored between people so that they might have a better relationship; it being one of the basics of a real relationship.

The pain I was experiencing at home was tremendous. I wasn't interested in determining blame or even in understanding all the nuances of the problems—it just hurt. It hurt all the time. Nothing I did or said helped the situation. All I could think about was "What is going on here? And "How much more can I take?" I had been taught that a wife should not leave the home for any reason, so one can imagine my shock upon hearing JW say in one of our first phone conversations:

"When you are in a tub of scalding hot water, you do not stay in the scalding water and say, ' I am committed to cleanliness.'"

Never had I heard such a statement from a Christian counselor or author! It was so foreign sounding that it did not even register in my mind for several seconds. I was ready to hear what I'd always heard before, "If you will just ______, then everything will be okay in your marriage." Various people in various ways had most always said the same thing when I asked for help-- "It is your fault that your husband is angry."

I took the advice given and as I already said, I begged God to do whatever He wanted to do in order to fix me. I took about 99% of the blame. (More on that later)

I could not believe my ears! Did JW just say what I thought he said? Was he saying I could leave from a painful situation? I had to give this some careful thought. I absolutely would not do such a thing quickly or lightly? After all, I was a pastor's wife and a full time minister.

It took more than five weeks of agonizing over this jewel before I got out of the scalding water. The pain was nearly unbearable, and trying to decide what to do was difficult. It hurt to be misunderstood, but it hurt more to live in hostility. With JW's encouragement, I kept trying to feel all feelings and to feel as badly as I needed to feel, while at the same time practicing coming and going in small increments—as little as one or two feet in a room. Sometimes I left the room, sometimes I went out to spend the night, until finally I went away to rest for a month at Margaret's apartment.

Leaving my home escalated the misunderstanding, rejection, and pain from my community. It seemed that only two or three people understood at all. JW said that by staying in a hostile environment I was allowing someone to hurt "a valuable me." I certainly did not recognize the depths of my value until much later, but I loved hearing him say that I was valuable, when so many were giving me the opposite message.

"You would jump out of a hot bathtub and say, "I don't like hot water and I won't be back until it is the right temperature."

"To have a healthy, strong relationship, both parties have to be free to come and go. If one cannot go, or let the other go, then he or she cannot love with *Agape* Love. Jesus went away at times from the hostility around Him. He also went away just to be by himself."

I began to see that for most of my marriage, I had lived in fear of going out and not returning on some schedule. I could trace it back to the early years when I allowed fear of disapproval, which could even be non-verbal, to control me. I realized that living from this and other fear based relating had caused me to stop acting like myself. I was not free to be who I am and I had to get out of the scalding water to work on something that was off-kilter inside me.

I could no longer hide from the community that everything was not okay at home. I was going to have to learn that I truly could be free to come and go, leave and return, regardless of any disapproval. I had to face that a fear-based relationship was not a real relationship at all.

"We are socialized out of moving around—'good kids sit still,' we are taught. We tend not to move when depressed. Unfreeze your body."

"You will have to speak to others and explain about your coming and going. Staying is not good for anyone."

"David communicated with Saul out of spear throwing range. (1 Samuel 26:13) You will make mistakes trying to say what you need to say, and when trying to do what you need to do. Others will not like the mistakes."

"Your husband will have hurt feelings, too. Let him be upset. You don't have to fix it. You or he may have to go away to process with someone else."

"If you were being yourself, you would leave. This *is* being yourself. You do not like being hurt and will remove yourself when hurt. The idea is to come and go. You can try explaining, but you do not have to finish discussions. You might leave too often for a while. It's okay to make mistakes. Go out, change your mind, then come back. Find yourself. What do you want? This is not about ending a marriage; it is about not allowing yourself to be hurt."

"In my experience, when a spouse leaves in order to try to get a message through to the other, it takes from six months to a year before the other hears the message. It will not be easy and it may not be heard at all."

When JW told me this, I did not believe him. I thought if I did something so drastic as leaving, that my message would be heard very quickly.

"Sometimes we have to say to another, 'You are hurting me and it seems that you don't care that you are hurting me.'"

"Allowing someone to hurt us destroys both their self esteem and ours."

"We had an old car with no heater. We were visiting my parents in the north. It was thirty degrees below zero. Some would say my wife was disloyal if she did not ride with me when my dad had a car with a heater. She rode with my dad. She was not disloyal, even if anyone had said she was."

In answer to my question about when to think about returning, JW said, " When the other person begins to say, 'I am dangerous to you sometimes and since I can't control that, you need to be away from me.' Then you will know that he is thinking of your pain and the message you are trying to give."

These jewels were foreign to me, yet so sensible. It was a very difficult thing to do. For years I had been taught, "You better stay under your umbrella of protection or else." There had been no place in my thinking to leave my home even for a short period. It was a very big step for me to practice coming and going. When I came back for Christmas, I stayed until March 1995, when I left again. (More on that later)

ON TRUST AND SAFETY

After I left that first month in 1994, Jim tried very hard to win me back, but from my viewpoint his words were not sinking in. It is so easy to say, "I love you." We do it all the time. But it can be confusing when words and actions don't always match. I was too broken and damaged to feel safe anymore and the dark storm clouds had destroyed my trust. Ambivalent feelings were very strong. JW had some good jewels for this paradox.

"Without trust it is hard to feel loved."

"There can be no true intimacy without trust and safety."

"Our identities are only open to those with whom we bond and whom we trust. Only those we trust can truly touch us deeply in our core self, our heart."

It seemed to me that JW meant by this jewel that we should be really open only to people whom we can trust to tell us rightly who we are. It also seemed to say that when we trust and bond wrongly with someone, or with someone who doesn't love us rightly, they can touch our core and tell us things that are not true about us. (This is certainly true when people abuse children.) As my understanding about safety grew, I began to acknowledge more quickly when I did not feel safe with someone and then I became better at taking action to take care of myself.

ON "NICE"

In the early months of correspondence with JW right after the conference, as I struggled with my questions about submission, rejection of the new information I'd learned, pain and no one to talk to about it, it was difficult to express the whirlwinds that sprung up in my mind about Jim and me because so much of our life together had been good. "Quite often," I told JW, "He can be nice to me. Why do I have so much pain?" I truly wanted to give Jim the benefit of the doubt. JW had some great words for my struggle:

"You say often, that in spite of the negatives, your husband can be very nice to you. You seem very affected by this and it makes it difficult for you to realize when he is not and remove yourself. I recommend that you do a word study through the scripture on the word 'nice.' Something so powerful needs a full understanding."

I laughed out loud because I immediately knew that this powerful word "nice" was not even in the Scriptures. I did not need to look it up.

He continued, "Niceness makes you feel guilty and crazy. It is obviously a very powerful and controlling force in your life."

I was startled to realize that I had used that word my whole life, and taught my own children, "Now, be nice!" JW went on to say,

"A problem with niceness is that it is judged ultimately by how the receiver likes it. This is one of the ways it makes you feel guilty or crazy. There is a bit of manipulation in it. An example is the phrase that some people use, 'I can't do anything right (nice enough) for you.' This statement indicates that their real reason for being nice is to get a response. They are not actually loving you unconditionally. Jesus did what he did because he was acting like Himself (love) and to do otherwise would violate his personhood. True *kindness* (the Scripture word) is of this nature—given because it was in the nature of the giver. If it is well received, that says something about the nature of the receiver. If it is received with hostility and meanness, it's the same. It says something about the receiver. Out of the heart the mouth speaks."

"Another belief you have about 'nice' is 'If I am just nice enough, everything will turn out right for everyone.'"

This jewel hit me hard. It was certainly very true that I believed this. It burned in my thoughts for many months and took a long, long time and lots of practice to undo the wrong belief.

"When someone is nice to you, you cannot be tough back (you have to be nice back) and that causes you to justify taking the hurt when they are not nice. You get paralyzed with fear."

"Most of us were raised to believe that it is not nice to ever hurt anyone. This is not the same as being loving and kind. Being nice feels like it's right but it may not be love. Sometimes love hurts and does not look or feel very nice. The Cross is an example of love that hurt. It did not look very nice of the Father."

JW was right. These jewels about "nice" impacted me greatly and I eliminated that word from my vocabulary and have used the word 'kind' in its place ever since. I worked diligently to get this new concept as part of my thinking and reacting, but it took a while before I was able to be tough when I needed to be tough.

ON PRIORITIES

One of the accusations I received from Jim and our community after leaving home that first time was that I did not have my priorities straight. "Why are you working on yourself and not your marriage? You're talking to that man on the phone and you should be going to marriage counseling," said someone in my community. Keeping priorities straight was another teaching that had been hammered into me. I understand that one has to go to work instead of golf all the time and that we have to put paychecks into the bank instead of gambling them away, but JW stirred up my thinking and I had to ponder the good Scriptural point that he makes:

"There is very little in Scripture that translates as 'priority.' In Scripture the idea is more like 'simultaneous'—'Love the Lord.... and your neighbor....' 'Submit yourselves one to another....' The American way seems to be, 'First do this, love this one, then if anything, or any time, is left I'll love the next one.' Sickness comes when we try to prioritize and stack. It extinguishes spontaneity and leads to exclusiveness. It is about as fun as eating all the flour, then eating the sugar next."

ON FEELINGS VS DESIRES

As I followed God's leading to feel every feeling as it came I had plenty to feel. Some days I felt angry at Jim, angry with Margaret for leaving me and angry with my community for not understanding. This did not mean that I would act out the anger on someone else, because I was committed to following my desires, not my feelings. If I was feeling rage at someone who had hurt me or misunderstood me, I felt those feelings privately or with someone I trusted. I screamed into my pillow or hit the couch or my mattress. One day I took a plastic bat and hit a pole in my basement until the bat broke into many pieces. I threw ice into the bathtub or off the back porch. I drew brightly colored pictures of my rage, feeling it all until it was over.

When I felt hurt or grief, I kept crying until the feelings were over. I did not suppress the feelings. If I had thoughts about doing something back to someone or at them, I did not act it out. I put the feelings into words in my journal, because following God's way was my true desire. Hurting someone back is not satisfying and JW told me many times to seek what satisfies, which are those things we truly desire.

"While you are looking for the things that satisfy, feel what you feel about them. It is satisfying to give life not destroy it. Even if it is difficult to feel your hurt and not take revenge, you will do these things because what we truly desire (what satisfies) is what motivates us. You won't act on the negative feelings. By just feeling them, they won't control you. Live by your true desires."

"Receiving and giving life are the truly satisfying things."

ON IDENTITY AND IDENTITY CHANGE

Often it felt to me that most of the people who were supposed to love me were deserting me or rejecting me at the time of my greatest need. I grew more uncertain of what to do with this mess. By now (March 1995) I had been back home for four months. During that time, right before Christmas, one of the women I was counseling had to go to the hospital. Her daughter was staying with us. When she returned, I knew I was going to have to leave again. Whatever God was doing in me, I could not process it at home. Hopeless despair set in until one day I said in our small group meeting, "I feel like a nobody with nowhere to go." I ran upstairs to my bedroom, crying. Joann came up to tell me that I could stay with her for a while. So I moved out again.

As I said earlier, during my pain and depression, JW sent me the manuscript for his book *The Red Dragon Cast Down*. I was reading it over and over because so much of it was new to me or was a new way of looking at old things I already knew. During this time alone at Joann's house is when God began to open up to me what was happening. This was when I realized how Margaret leaving was a parallel to what happened to me at fourteen, while at the same time dealing with the messed up marriage.

For the next three months, God, JW, and a few remaining friends and family supported me through what JW calls in *The Red Dragon Cast Down* an "identity change." This is a process whereby a person relinquishes an old identity before finding a new one. In normal chronological growth, people pass naturally from one stage to the other at the transformation points in natural human maturity—infant to child, child to adult, adult to parent, etc. Emotional development can be arrested by trauma, or by missing the normal identity change point from some kind of lack, which then causes emotional maturity and chronological maturity to be out of synchronization and the person does not progress through the stages of maturity. For me, the rape at fourteen had arrested part of my emotional development.

When an ID change does not take place at the proper age because of some lack, or a trauma has occurred, the person needs healing and help through to the next stage. JW calls this a *redemptive* identity change. Because it did not come as part of the normal growth processes, the person became separated somehow from part of his or her complete identity. This redemptive change cannot be accomplished by anyone alone; it takes the community. The person needs help because a redemptive or corrective identity change requires a crisis of death to the old identity in order to move into the new one.

Since the traumatized person is avoiding pain in that area where a lack or a trauma occurred, a separation from that part of his or her identity involved in the trauma takes place inside and an emotional barrier is set up that closes off that part of the identity. Emotional growth is arrested. In addition to the pain of the lack or trauma itself, a lie or distortion is believed against the true identity in the heart, which creates more pain that he or she will avoid. It is very painful to lose part of oneself. It is very painful to try to live out a lie against one's true self. This buried pain and its attending lies have to be faced and felt in order to move on to the next maturity stage. As I was discovering, when one begins to feel the pain, it gets worse. Dying is hard; despair can be very heavy, especially when experienced without enough support.

(For a very detailed description, see Appendix of Guidelines in *The Red Dragon Cast Down*, pp. 324-326, paraphrased here.)

Being nearly alone in my despair created a double bind as I faced the effects of the rape while at the same time losing my marriage. The trauma had caused part of my identity to be separated and shut off from growing any further. That part of me was "stuck" at fourteen in the grip of painful lies, most of which I had not even identified yet. JW was my principle supporter and that was usually only once a week by phone.

"ID changes require disintegration of the self. This can be very terrifying as everything and all the sense of who you are collapses. The old must die to have the new. The main ingredient is to be around people who will tell you who God says you are. They will help renew your mind while you are collapsed. Do not fear the falling apart. Major problems come from fighting. Do not make any life decisions during it. Navigate moment by moment. Some will think as things improve, 'It is all done, now get on with things.'"

I stumbled almost blindly, step by step through this disintegration. There were not many around who would tell me who God says I am. During these weeks alone at Joann's I had three or four friends and three of my children that were at least willing to talk with me. I hardly had words for what was happening. It was not easy to "study and learn" the process during so much pain, depression and failure. I needed many jewels. It would not be until much later that I could describe how I had grown past the "stuck" place and began to settle into a "new identity."

"Surround yourself with people who will tell you who you are."

"You have lost yourself by listening to and believing people who tell you who you are not. Stand on what the ones who truly know you are saying."

"If you needed something emotionally in the past from someone, it is too late now to get it and resolve the hurt. You needed it then. It is like Mary when Lazarus died—'Lord if only you had been here....' Now Jesus has to do something different."

When the trauma happened, I needed something from my parents that they were not equipped to give. I needed kindness and support now from my husband and community, but I was getting rejection. JW told me that it was too late to get what I had needed before. I couldn't go back and start over either event; I could only go where Jesus was leading now.

"At night, review what was satisfying that day. What makes going to bed okay? Was it a child you saw, some food you ate, flowers, a tree, a book you read? This will help the depression."

I salvaged some of my worst days by thinking of my grandchildren. Wanting to see them grow up was the only thing that kept me going. Being with them was very satisfying.

"Feed the new identity as it grows. What satisfies is what feeds it. Try things. If it doesn't satisfy you, don't keep it."

"Keep studying yourself—watch how you respond, instead of just responding."

"Tell others your story as you want to tell. It will become more solid."

"Pay attention to things that people have told you that are negative in your personality. Reframe them to decontaminate them. Modify or erase erroneous labels. For example—other people say you interrupt--I see this as eagerness."

"God already gave you a new name. Believe it and practice using it with safe people."

"Discover Barbara-like effects on the world. A dog doesn't have to worry about being doggish. God doesn't have to worry about having Godish effects on the world. What are some of your effects on the world, your characteristics that no one has seen? Celebrate your discoveries. Later you won't have to worry about them."

It was difficult to look for new aspects of myself that were Barbara-like, but I made the effort to ask myself now and then, "What is like me here?" One example that JW told me was, "It is like you to hurt when someone does not want to be with you. It is like you to hurt over all these losses."

As I struggled to hold on and not give up, JW encouraged me each week:

"You have been afraid of collapse. Don't try to stop it or escape it. Let it be. Disaster comes from trying to stop or fix it."

"When you stop trying to stop it or fix it—you are free!"

During this period, not only was my marriage deteriorating, but other important relationships were as well. I was continually being rejected or misunderstood by people who were close to me. It really hurt to be accused of things that were not true. Some of the accusations made were that I was self-deceived and did not know what I was doing. JW told me,

"One of the scariest things is to be self-deceived. Someone can always make that point. There is a level of trust some of us can get to—for us to trust God more than our own mind. All you have is God. You love Him. If you are self deceived, He will use your self-deception, bless it, even make a fool out of you. You are His to do that with. If your mind fails you, your failed mind is what you have.

I heard accusations that I was in denial. JW assured me:

"I have not found you to be a person who lives in denial. You seem to take what you hear and try to learn from it. That is why you have often felt beaten up in churches or other Christian meetings. Most speakers are sending 'denial bombs' at their audiences to try and jolt them out of complacency or unbelief or apathy. This makes for strong words that will "bombard" any denial they are in about their condition or actions. You didn't need the bombs, so you just felt beaten up."

"You are really vexed at being mistaken for someone else, not known as who you are. ('How long have I been with you and you still don't know me?' John 14:9.)'"

"Not being known for yourself is painfully intolerable."

About the relationships I had lost, JW encouraged me that there was nothing I could do to redeem them, only God knew what the outcomes would be.

"There has to be a death of a relationship to get a new one. Life is not guaranteed by the death. It has to be up to God. Do not try to revive the old ones. Ask God for the grace to see how bad everything is. It takes blind faith and this is scary."

I often allowed the numerous rejections, misunderstandings, and accusations to batter me. Back and forth my thoughts flowed as I worried that my accusers were right, even though I felt deep in my heart they were not. It was very painful to be separated from so many in my time of need. Was I sinning to be out of my home? Was I making mountains out of molehills? Should I go back no matter what? Was I just having a pity party or going through menopause? JW commented on this:

"When you are accused of having a 'pity party,' that is to put you down. This is just one of the many things you will be accused of."

"When you know yourself better, you will know what is yours to take and believe from accusers and what are your accusers' internal dialogues about themselves. Then, if you have the privilege, you can turn them back to their hurt and sit with them in their pain.

"Others are telling you that you are playing games in all this. I know three people who say you do not do that—Me, your son, Bobby, and God."

"It is alright to defend yourself when necessary. You are worth defending. What you cannot take is untakeable. You cannot get tough enough or well-enough to take it. It is like you to hurt when wounded, attacked, or rejected for being yourself."

"God bears the unbearable. Learn to be fearless. Explore the world. Find the things about yourself that are so unique about you that they would not fit anyone else so you've hidden them away."

"Someone who sees you as you really are will tell what is <u>really</u> there, 'good and/or bad'." (I thought of the story, *The Emperor's New Clothes*)

In these interactions with people in my immediate community, JW helped me to see that God was in all the circumstances and he helped me not to look at results, but to keep my eyes on God and what He was doing in everyone. I was not the only one getting lessons from God.

"God is the archer and we are His arrows. We are all <u>bent</u> arrows. Our hope is not that some day we will be straight arrows;

but rather that our Archer is so good He can shoot bent arrows around corners with perfect precision. He knows we are but dust. He will not fail to touch you through negative relationships. He will not fail to touch others back and forth in your community. Some who claim to be healthy are self-deceived."

I liked this analogy so well that in May 1996 I wrote in my journal about the dusty bent arrow I am. It was very freeing to look at myself this way—all is in God's hands and He will take care of everything His way.

The Dusty Bent Arrow

I am a dusty bent arrow
Very crooked and marred.
The quiver is getting older
Nicked, beaten and scarred.

Arrows should be straight,
Finely honed and such.
Standing tall in the quiver
Awaiting the hunter's touch.

How can the hunter
Darting deer bring down
Except the arrow fly truly
And not around and 'round?

Only arrows quite perfect
With balance straight and so
Can pierce the heart of the hunted
When loosed from the bow.

"But!" cries the Lord of the Hunters,
"The arrow's not the prize.
Bent dusty arrows are best—
The trueness comes from MY eyes."

"Crooks and mars in the arrow
Are used for and by me.
Going perfectly 'round a corner
Flying straight to what *I* see."

JW's jewels about identity continued.

"Satan attacks us at the point where we will experience our deepest identity. Since loving and bonding are your true identity, you will flourish in Christ. So Satan wants to hurt that in you the most with all kinds of accusations that you are not loving, but rather that you are hurtful, hard, mean; thus denying your real identity if you believe him."

"Unless the enemy is not doing well today, he will have set it up to be able to destroy all the people involved here, you, your husband, your friends, your family. Destroying one will destroy the others. Without God's intervention, it will work. Satan likes to win. Pray that his trap backfires."

"When you are 'defenseless' and all your fears have come true, you will be a bonding nurturing, loving person regardless of the flak you get."

"When going through an identity change, you mustn't exclude any parts of yourself. Bring in all the pieces--the pain from the rape, the failed marriage, the lost friends. Don't hide the rejected pieces. They are hidden by defense mechanisms because you think you are bad.

The part that feels the most pain is the "bad" part. That part carries the pain from all the rejection you have received. You will learn to accept her and do something about her pain for healing. Take the pain to Jesus to resolve."

"You can only do what you know right now. You have to have help from ones who love and know you. It is too hard to go to God by yourself.

"When you are on the other side, you will be less upset by responses to you being yourself, but it will still hurt when others don't like it. It is true that some won't like you when you do Barbara-like things."

Many times JW gave me a special jewel by praying for me:

"Jesus is dancing around you and celebrating you."

"Lord, help her to live in a world that does not fit well with Barbara-like effects and change her world through her effects."

"You truly are Bringer of Joy."

I asked JW one day, "Will I like the new me?" It's hard to put into words what his answer meant to me. He answered, "If you like God."

ON FEAR

Most of my life I had considered myself a person with few fears. I was adventurous and self-confident. I did not understand that many, many fears could be emotional. JW told me that during this time, I should be finding my worst fears, because they all were going to come true. These are some jewels I heard about that along the way.

"At the end of your identity change, (the dying process through which I was going in order to get healing from the rape and the pain in my marriage) after all the fears you have had come true, they will turn to ashes and blow away. You will no longer walk in fear."

"You seem to be making good progress on discovering your fear. I am always sure that our worst fear is that of being our true selves as God created us. For you that would be the fear of truly being loving and bonding with freedom because you are afraid of what others will see and misunderstand, reject and attack. I'm not sure that is right on, but it is close.

The love you feel with your love bond to Margaret is characteristic of you and your relationships. Your love for me and for others is also. This is greatly threatening to those who hoard fear, and it totally enrages that Old Red Dragon who will tear at you with all his fierceness every time you try to express love—which is why you fear."

Since I had listened so long to others telling me I was not loving, and, leaving Jim looked unloving, at times I still struggled with what to believe. JW admonished me,

"Stop fearing that you are not a loving person. Either God has made you one or you are not one."

From *The Red Dragon Cast Down* I read:

"Fear is avoidance-based thinking and behavior. Fear causes us to train the spotlight of our awareness on the things that can hurt us. This is a life of worry. Diminishing returns from fear demand greater threats to achieve the same response. People are easily controlled by whomever they fear. They can think of nothing else. Even within this fear dynamic there is hope, because God is the most frightening power we know. Wisdom, (the way out of fear) begins with fearing God. The first words out of His mouth, however, are usually, 'Fear not!'" * Page 124

I was getting the picture that most everything boiled down to either love or fear. That made it easier to discern what was going on around me. It was not easy to acknowledge that I had a fear bond with my husband when I wanted to believe we'd had a love bond.

"An unhealthy fear bond or trauma bond occurs when someone becomes emotionally attached to something or someone who is hurting them."

JW helped me see that even churches, families, organizations have either fear or love bonds.

"Churches form using either fear bonds or love bonds, which produce either fear or love dynamics in the congregation." **The Red Dragon* Page 135

"Fears should neither control us or be dismissed. Fear bonds are broken by identifying them---and then letting God heal the injury that caused the fear. Face and move beyond your fears."

"You cannot build a healthy bond on fear. Fear equals fear. Trust and love are made differently from fear."

As understanding and healing took place, I began to feel freer. I could not go back to living from fear.

"Now you're emotionally allergic to trafficking in fear. You want to lead others to a different way."

ON FAILURE

Fear of failure was another fear in my heart of which I was unaware. It was not on my agenda to fall completely apart, be deeply depressed and have such a messed up marriage, especially after walking with God for many years and being in ministry. Most anything I had ever tried to do, I had accomplished. I was what some call a "high achiever." I always took my frustrations and pains to God, asking Him to change me in any way that would make me more like Him. I truly lived a good life. I did everything I heard, read or learned to try to make my marriage work. I was relying on God. But failure was looming largely on the horizon, and that wasn't supposed to happen.

These great jewels were and still are some of my favorites. I taped several of them onto my mirror so I would hide them deeply in my heart. They really did make a deep change in my every day journey.

My favorite: "No one can talk me into picking up my van. If I really believe I can't, I won't try. If I try—I think I can."

This jewel taught me to quit trying to make things work. JW very often used the physical world to illustrate a Spiritual or emotional truth. For weeks when I was frustrated over messes that kept occurring as I walked through this depression and ID change, I would picture myself trying to pick up my car. Sometimes I didn't remember that I couldn't do it until after I had tried to "pick up my car" by trying to make things work out. Eventually, I came to believe and rest that I could not change things by myself, even with God.

(The following is another jewel that JW does not recommend for new or immature Christians. Take it prayerfully, as it was given.)

"When we are in a loving context, we learn from mistakes because we do not have to cover them up—it's ok to have them. There is no condemnation given out for mistakes or wrongs. There may be consequences and disciplines, but not condemnation. It's ok to not be good all the time. You need to come to the end of being good, so you can more deeply know God's grace and forgiveness. Go out and do something bad. (This is the healthy thing to be learned while young.)"

Besides not quite believing someone would give this advice, I was very glad I had already done some bad things. It would be very difficult to go do something bad, deliberately, as an adult.

"The first step to freedom is to know what things don't work. The second is to despair that they will ever work."

Because I tried so hard to make things better, JW told me many times that I believed that my words or my love could change things. That was a very subtle and deep-seated lie in my thinking. I did not know that I believed this lie about my marriage, my ministry with women, or even my children. I had taken some Scriptures like 1 Peter and others about love, coupled with much "how-to" literature, and tried to get my words and love just right so that circumstances would change. JW set me straight:

"Your love does not make it better, nor is it capable of producing results. You cannot love enough to change things. Even God knows that His great love will not change everyone. Stop caring so much about 'results'."

"Sometimes people believe 'If you just loved me enough I'd be ok.' Others believe if I just _______enough, everything will be ok.' You cannot love anyone enough to make them ok, so stop believing that you can. It does not make you a failure. It brings rest."

"Your can never say your words correctly enough nor love enough to help some people."

I had people in my life who were greatly disappointed in my failures, to say the least. I was supposed to be the human rock, not only of my family, but my community. Now that rock looked like the sand it truly was. I received criticism for my actions of moving out, crying all the time, taking medication, and seeming to be sinning because my actions looked so crazy. JW spoke to this aspect of failure:

"You will be free when you know 'we can't get it right'. When someone is disappointed with you, saying something is wrong with you, they are implying you <u>could</u> get it right. It is ok to be wrong, because we cannot do it right in and of ourselves. If when I get to Heaven, I find I had much of anything right about God I will be amazed. Fearing to do the wrong thing is one of Satan's traps. Undo the trap by knowing you can't get it right (more on this later)."

I had to chew on this jewel. As I did, it brought rest and freedom. Not only did I not have to take another's accusation or disappointment, I could know that they were putting a load on me that was not mine to carry. It was another way of combating that old thinking about performance based living.

"Insight (knowledge, teaching, words, love) is not enough for change and healing. If someone is starving, insight won't feed them."

"Get comfortable with the reality that you will fail. Learn to live with limitations. Limitations are not bad and neither is failure. Remember God knows we are but dust. (Remember the dusty bent arrow?) Don't assume that He has expectation and gets disappointed in us."

These jewels were so comforting and freeing.

ON FEELINGS

During the time that many friends seemed to be deserting me in my need and Margaret came to a place that she felt for her own good that she had to pull back from being with me, it felt like the absolute end of the world. I could not bear to have that attention and love from her removed, but I was dragging her through painful places that were far beyond her ability to handle and were not her job to do. My depression deepened. I could barely make it to school (work), I could not eat, and hopeless despair was my constant companion.

Since I seemed to be looking at losing Margaret as the reason for the pain, JW had to remind me many times that the depth of pain I was feeling was not only about Margaret. She was a parallel for losing the comfort from my mother after the rape. God was using the situation with Margaret to tap into the buried feelings from the past. I was feeling what I did not feel at the time it happened. These jewels were very difficult to internalize, and it took some time for me to truly understand how painful that part of the trauma had been. Understanding that some present pain is amplified by past pain is a very important aspect of healing past traumas or neglects. JW helped me to look at overwhelming emotions in a different way.

"Some of these feelings you are having about Margaret (and others) are too big to be about the present. You have not known Margaret long enough for them to be this big. This is a signal that they are about past pain that is unresolved."

"The more unrealistic and unfitting to the present reality that your feelings are, the more it shows the extent to which they are from the past. Put the feelings where and on whom they belong."

"When we are living normally with emotions, any emotion last about 90 seconds. This would not be true when learning to feel them, but is the goal to move towards as a normal length."

"Feelings are energy, not personality traits. Don't take any condemnation for having them."

ON PLAYING (AFTER HURT, CRY AND COMFORT)

The deeper my despair grew during the aloneness, rejection and misunderstanding, the more JW told me I had to play. That seemed strange, since the picture I had of depression was to lie in a dark room with covers over my head. I never really did that, but I was spending hours sitting inside with my Bible and journal. It was very difficult to begin "playing," but I bought an old bicycle and began to ride around the apartment where I was staying with Joann. I also started walking with Joann. When I had my lunch break at school, I would stand in the window and let the sun shine on my face for as long as I could. These different activities helped push away the dark clouds.

"God's blessing is rest. (Play) You must get out and move around."

"You need to play, especially when working on hard things."

"Get more miserable, then go play. We can't make God move. When we feel powerless and stuck, the reasonable thing to do is to go out and play. Get to where you play two-three hours per day."

I'd never heard that before—go play when I'm miserable and stuck?

ON POWER and BLAME (From The Red Dragon Cast Down)

I loved what JW wrote about power and blaming. It was another way to look at control, a much-debated issue in my marriage. This was another debate I had inside with God and myself about whether I was crazy or not. I took blame that I was controlling when I didn't think I was. As I've said before, it was often hard for me to "trust my gut" about my feelings. I wanted clarity on this issue because I felt that the accusations did not fit. Taking untrue blame was partly a result of my rape and partly the lack of boundaries in my marriage. I put this section here because it was a big key to my healing and freedom to be myself.

"In many families the one with the power (usually Dad) does not suffer (feel pain.) Children (and others without power) learn to believe—If I have power, I will not have pain." * Page 176

"If a child cries himself to sleep alone, he will think, 'If I have power, I will not have pain.'" * Page 176

What I take from these quotes is that children in homes where power is misused and not shared lovingly learn to want power the wrong way. They want power so they can control and get their own way—thus have no pain. They want it to do exactly what was done to them—overpower others in order to feel powerful. The result is a person full of fear and anger.

"Fear and anger are two major symptoms of people who feel a lack of power." * Page 169

"People who blame and control others feel powerless. They think of relationships as power equations, so they blame to feel powerful and diminish the other. Blaming others ensures the one blaming is always right and they get their way."

"It is usually the person who feels the most out of control who tries to control a situation. They try to extend fear bonds because they feel powerless and fearful. They loudly accuse the other of being controlling." * Paraphrased, Page 178

"Providing your children with power and teaching them how to use it well, is a major form of Satan-proofing your children. Powerful children can do hard things. Building powerful love bonds is how we build powerful children."
* Page 168

"Three very good questions to help evaluate our use of power and help build it properly into our children: What kind of power did Dad have? More importantly, what got him to use it? What induced him to share his power? Fathers should share their power lovingly." * Paraphrased pages 133,134

"How do we share our power with our children? Help them achieve their goals, give them some power over their environment, teach them to think wisely, solve problems on their own, plan things and learn to live with limitations."
* Paraphrased page 172

As I pondered these sections of *The Red Dragon*, I realized that my father had for the most part shared his power lovingly and that I had been taught most of the ideas here. This helped me have a better balance about my "high achievements" and learning to live with my limitations, to be proud in the right way. It helped me understand my husband's ways better because I knew he had grown up in a family where dad did not share his power lovingly, where he was not helped to achieve goals or solve problems very well. I had always tried to understand him, knowing his past, but that had often caused me to take negatives from him instead of being objective when necessary. I could understand him better, but at the same time I had to stop taking blame from him and others when it was not true.

Another aspect of power involves how power, love and fear affect the way others see Jesus in us:

"The power of the Gospel is no greater than the strength of its bonds. When someone sees that our love for the Lord is greater than our fear, they are more likely to want to know Jesus." * Paraphrased Page155

This reminded me about the many Christian martyrs and how their lack of fear facing torture and death encouraged those watching to come to Jesus.

I received another jewel over the phone about blaming. It concerned my self-blame. For years I had taken the blame upon myself, as most women do, that the rape was my fault somehow. JW helped me see the lie in that as well.

"If you (Barbara) blamed yourself for the rape, then that means that you think you could have prevented or changed the outcome. That is not true."

It's difficult to express the comfort I felt in knowing that it was not my fault. Slowly but surely God was healing different areas of these deep wounds. It was now over a year since I'd met Dr. Wilder.

PART THREE

THE HEALINGS COME

ON THE HEALING, March 1995

Most of the time that I'd spent talking and corresponding with JW had been filled with tremendous pain. I had learned many of the jewels that JW gave me. I had practiced feeling pain until it stopped and had continued searching for unresolved things from the past. Now JW began to encourage me that it was time to resolve some of the separated places that were unhealed and unconnected inside. Because of the rape and subsequent loss of my mother's comfort, there was a barrier keeping me from growing past that time and taking on the next maturity stage for my life. JW saw me halfway into the Elder stage, but the unresolved pain was a deterrent to further maturity. I had to get into all the feelings I did not feel at fourteen and let Jesus heal completely. JW advised:

"Tell God how bad it is, how long it has been. If others don't listen, tell them over and over how needy you are. If they don't like it, say it anyway. The words that you are hearing from others now are words for feelings you did not allow yourself to feel at fourteen -- 'You are bad; I am angry with you; I don't want to be with you; It is not ok to not be ok; you have to hide how you really feel: hurry up and get over it, etc.' You must separate the past pain of losing your mother and friends from the present pain of losing Margaret, Jim and friends so you can process it all. Tell God, 'I am ready to be healed.' Keep telling Him the truth, how bad it feels. You have known Jesus deeply these last years and now you are better able to face and feel what you have to."

"At the end of childhood, about age thirteen, one should know what satisfies and how to get those things without qualms. Between thirteen and twenty we should learn to help three to four others get satisfaction at the same time as ourselves. That is like when two or more people that are in disagreement can compromise in a way that all are okay with the decision. In some ways your progress was halted at fourteen. You've acted the adult and the elder, but you did it best when you kept it separated from yourself. You could satisfy yourself *or* three to four others. When this is all resolved you will be able to do both *and*." (See *Life Model* for a complete discussion on the stages of life.)

Since connecting past pain to the present and resolving it was a big part of my healing journey, I wrote this poem in my journal in March 1995 about wanting to find the damaged part that was stuck at fourteen and have God heal her. I was learning that all of us have some part of ourselves that got damaged and buried. God wants to heal and redeem all of it, and I wanted Him to do it.

Connecting

Lord, I come to ask you now
Make my outside more like You.
I wish to shed your love abroad
And have my actions be like new.

You know the things I do not like
You know how others I annoy.
Burn your fire within my soul
And make my life another story.

When my soul was shred that day
The walls went up my pain to hide.
The message came both loud and clear
"Never feel the other side."

You sent someone with perfect skill
You sent the perfect parallel.
Each and every step You made
Fit the past exactly well.

Oh, the pain and suffering
That pounded all through this heart of mine.
When you made the actions here and now
Open the darkness to let You shine.

The only way to out is through.
No longer may I hide away
All the pain from then and now
May never ever covered stay.

Now I see the walls were used
To cover up the pain unfelt.
They made the actions twisted be
Hiding me until they melt.

I need the walls to keep me in
The message said, 'I need to be.'
Never let them know the pain.
No one hears or wants to see.

The growth was stopped and disappeared
The child so free was stabbed and dead.
She used to come for comfort near
But now she'd stay inside her head.

Tonight I saw the mystery,
The whys of all the actions shown.
The free one died and covered up
To keep me safe 'til I was grown.

The things I'm told by Dr. Jim
Explain the ways to bridge the past.
They make the present pain so real
Bring healing to my soul at last.

One day when whole and healed I am
He says the walls will broken be.
When you heal that child you'll bring
And set her free herself to be.

I was beginning to see myself as I saw my little granddaughter, Erica—loved, carefree, unafraid to ask or tell her needs, free to be who she is—an adorable, wonderful, secure, imperfect, outgoing, loving, bonding person.

ON GETTING TO KNOW THE LOST PARTS OF MYSELF

One evening during the three months I was living with Joann, after time with JW and writing to God in my journal, again asking Him to please do something about all this pain, I sensed that He was showing me something inside. I was thinking about the rape and all the new ways I had been looking at it and feeling about it. Writing the poem and seeing that younger part of myself as being like my granddaughter gave me the picture I needed to uncover and accept this part. It seemed that God was showing me a picture of the fourteen year old me, deeply buried, covered in blackness. I could see her better now, as He showed me that she was the new name He had already given me—"Bringer of Joy." She was not completely clear, but I could see her as she had been before the rape: carefree, loving, bonding and joyful.

When I met JW, God had already given me my new name, Bringer of Joy. At the time, I hardly looked and felt like a bringer of joy. God told me to sign that name all the time as the salutation of my journal. It was a giant step of faith to begin doing that, only out of obedience and faith, just because

He said it. A long time went by before I even told anyone that He had given me a new name. Now God was making the faith step more real in my experience. In the next few days I wrote Bringer of Joy (myself) many letters. I saw better how my mother had continued to try love me, but I was so damaged I did not let her in. During those days of prayer, study and healing it also became clear to me that "we" must never again take ALL the blame in a relationship. In my mind I saw myself holding Bringer of Joy (BOJ as I called her), comforting her; I shared her pain and talked to her. I told her how sharing pain means you are very valuable.

JW's next jewels were about BOJ.

"You have a bright fourteen year old inside, and you would be dead if not for her. Let her heal and grow." Touched again by his understanding and love, I asked, 'You like me, don't you?' JW quickly responded, 'Oh, you better believe it. You're wonderful.'"

JW knew most of my self-condemning opinions, often believed because of others' accusations and put-downs. He liked to turn them into positives and see them through God's eyes. When he did that it was so encouraging:

"Let me help you reframe your trait of opinionated/dogmatic—your bright fourteen year old figures out what is true and unless a substantially better way or offer can be proven to her, she won't take it. She analyzes it and checks it out and puts it to the fire. She won't be easily persuaded or sweet-talked because of that trauma. I bet you haven't been raped again because of her strength. I know you have been raped emotionally, but that will be changing now."

But the days of agony, tears, anger and feeling pain were far from over. Hours later, I was back in it. I continually turned to Jesus, rehearsing the "fellowship of His suffering" and that whole passage of Philippians 3. Passage after passage of Scripture opened up to me in new ways in the next weeks. I devoured parts of Isaiah. I marked dates in my Bible for when God spoke to me. Isaiah 30:20, 21; 41:9, 10; 42:7; 45:2, 3; 49:15, 16, the end of 23; 54:4, 5, 11; 56:1, 2, 7; 58:6, 12. With Isaiah 58:12 God gave me another new name: Repairer of the Breach. I had no idea what that meant for several years. As best I can see at this time it has something to do with helping others find and heal their separated parts.

Colossians 1:24 became a favorite: "Now I rejoice in my sufferings for your sake, and in my flesh I do my share on behalf of His body (which is the church) in filling up that which is lacking in Christ's afflictions." I was honored to have any part in helping His church. Other passages such as Romans 8, Galatians 6, II Corinthians 1 and 1 Peter 4 brought me comfort. I was refreshed to remember how well He understands all the feelings we have and how non-condemning He is. How faithful are His promises.

A few weeks later, as I pondered the attributes that I wanted to see come from all this mess, the Lord Jesus showed me that I already had them buried deep inside. "'Bringer of Joy' has them, though they were misused, abused, or buried,'" He spoke to my heart. "She is loving, nurturing and kind. She is loyal and persevering in the face of rejection. She is strong and courageous. She is full of joy and a joy to others." Then in my mind I saw Him take a black curtain (the rest of the cloudiness) off of BOJ. Light shone all around and from her. For a long period there in my room I sat in the Presence of God, worshipping Him for His grace and mercy and the gift of healing. After the quiet awe, He took me to 2 Timothy 4:16-18: "At my first defense no one supported me, but all deserted me; may it not be counted against them. But the Lord stood with me , and strengthened me, in order that through me the proclamation might be fully accomplished..."

But--the pain continued--and the healing went three steps forward, two steps back.

ON BEING HELD

JW helped me grieve in several different ways. He knew my body was suffering from the strain as much as my heart was. He reminded me how important it was to feel and grieve the pain of lack surrounding my trauma.

"Remember that Margaret's love thawed much of your pain so that you would be aware enough of it to grieve. Grieve some more that you had the comfort from Margaret, but have not had <u>any</u> for a month now. Without some comfort you are not going to make it. You need someone to hold you every day. It has to be someone with whom you have a deep love bond. It won't make it hurt less, but it will be 'nutrients'. Your mother would be best. And do <u>not</u> be with anyone toxic or unsafe."

That very night that JW told me I needed to be held, God brought a miracle. Greg and Chris, my son and daughter-in-law, "just happened" to come by Joann's house to see me. I tearfully and humbly asked Greg if would hold me. I sat in Greg's lap for over an hour while he prayed spiritual warfare for me. What a blessing and what relief to feel comforted and cared for, and held!

God brought some other holding time with my son, Bobby, as well as from two friends, Mary Jo and Linda. It was such a blessing to have them help me and be willing to do such a "strange" thing. Another week God brought special comfort when my daughter, Jodi, came to visit from Texas.

Having these people minister to me brought enough strength that I felt I could make the trip to visit my mother who still lived in Oak Ridge. When I told her one of the reasons I was there was to sit in her lap and get comforted, without even asking for explanations, she sat down in her rocking recliner, took me, her fifty-two year old daughter into her lap and rocked me. We talked of many things as I cried upon her shoulder. I don't remember what the topics were, but I know the subject of my old trauma was not part of the discussion. I only wanted to think about all the good things she and my daddy had done for me and feel her blessings upon me.

To this day, when I remember or realize again all the good things that Mother or Daddy did for me through the years, I make a special effort to tell them. These memories far outweigh that time when they did not have the resources to bring me through the trauma. It was very comforting and healing to have this time with her and the others who did not desert me. This poem from my journal helped me express this time of healing.

Living Water

Long I faithed your living water
Long I waited cup held out
Asking, faithing, overflow me
Cleanse away my every doubt.

Long I sat at the well and waited
Long I told you of my love.
Trusting, speaking that you show me
The River flowing from above.

Now I'm understanding better.
Now I see the living well.
The rivers of your living water
Are really tears that flowed and fell.

No one likes to see the pain, Lord.
Some get up and leave the room.
Others hurt and cry there with me
Seeing hope within the gloom.

Being strong is not the way
Nor gushing out the love inside.
Pain and love go hand in hand
Being torn open turns the tide.

Long awaited gushing rivers
Long awaiting healing complete
Let the flow be from your hand, Lord
Keep me feeling, opened, deep.

Send the ones who need the river
Send them all you have for me.
There is plenty for them all, Lord
Let them each Your glory see.

ON KEEPING ON

Continual encouragement came over the phone lines every time I talked with JW as God moved me through various stages of healing. JW reminded me that everything does not change after an ID crisis. I would still basically be the same person, but would have more freedom and less fear. I would be able to express myself better and not take accusations and rejection as deeply. I would always be the dusty bent arrow--and needy.

Again: "Keep feeling the feelings. Go slowly and don't deal with what you are not ready to deal with. Wait for the right timing and when you feel safe enough. If you think a rattlesnake is in a box, you don't take the top off until you are ready to deal with it."

"When you come back from the dead, you are still needy and needing people. That is who you are—a needy person—needing them even if they are not there, not listening and rejecting you. Be whatever is there, even if you get flak and accusations. You are the image of God. He feels the same. So many do not listen to Him. They deny needs and that is like rebellion against God. We are dependent creatures who continuously need one breath at a time. Denying needs makes us hide."

JW felt strongly about not denying needs.

"Denial of needs falsely sanctifies Western independence and individuality. It is rebellion against God that denies our nature as dependent creatures who continuously need one breath at a time. . . When Christians deny their need for one another, they encourage fear-based church dynamics. Their needs, they fear will bring them rejection. Thus they hide from others." * Page 136 *The Red Dragon*

"What did Jesus do when He was needy? In the garden He asked three times for the disciples to pray with Him. He sweat blood and cried out to the Father."

Although I was getting a glimpse of the end of the tunnel, the pain continued, bringing with it more self doubts and struggles. Accusations hammered at me from many people because I had moved out of my home. I constantly questioned myself. *How do I know reality, make sense of all this? What is true? What do I do? Am I hearing God? How do I know if I should go back or not?* JW's jewels continued:

"Will you allow others to stop you from being yourself? Will you say who you are even if no one listens? It is all right to be confused. Others want answers now and they have a timetable that is up to *their* standards of satisfaction. You can take it by not fighting the pain. A little bit of self-protection is okay, too. When falsely accused, explore and consider the accusation or input, then keep it if it feels right and if it doesn't, don't keep it. You can say something like, 'What you are accusing me of is not me, but I'm sorry you feel that way.'"

At one point I received so much flak from others that my body literally went numb one night. It felt like the time I got so scared while talking to

Jim. This was one of my lowest days. I called Bobby and he said I should call JW even though it was an unscheduled day. JW lovingly reassured me:

"It is okay to be numb because you are overwhelmed by too much at once. You are sensitive and loving and the world is not good to people like that. You are bravely feeling your feelings and people will run and will poke at you. You seem yet to think there is something you can handle. Seeing your mother opened you up more and softened you so that the blows are harder to take. Most of the pain is present pain now and hurts a lot. Feel today's pain today."

"Let no one intimidate you. You do not have to prove anything. They will be demanding, but you cannot prove anything. They will be anxious and tell you that you are bad and untrustworthy by taking everyone out on thin ice. You used to claim to know where you were going. You do not have to give them the privilege of your insides to stomp on."

After talking with JW, I called Bobby again. His words were extra balm that soothed my aching wounds. "I have a picture of you as a leper, with open sores. Your friends have called you unclean, but Jesus is not repulsed. He will touch your wounds and heal them." I thought of the verse in Isaiah 61:1, and I could see Jesus embracing the lepers he met (Matthew 8:3). Jesus touches sores without reservation.

ON THINGS THAT WON'T CHANGE AFTER AN IDENTITY CHANGE

The negatives from my community did not end as the weeks went by. I doubt my progress was very evident yet, plus I didn't see very many people during this time at Joann's. JW elaborated on what would and would not change as God put me back together. It would take time to see what was different or what remained the same. He encouraged me to take all the time needed.

"When someone is put back together after a disintegration, it doesn't guarantee that all is back together correctly. Some old coping methods can still be used for a while. As children we rely on ourselves for repair. During redemptive disintegration there is no justifying of oneself possible. You can't say if you are good or bad. The way you are, the effects you have are God's. At that time of despair you don't know who you are and you can't figure it out. You must have around you ones who just care for you, whether they say anything or not--they just care for and love you. Your identity is continuing to grow and will grow back correctly as time passes: 'My, I'm loveable and it's beyond my understanding or capacity to figure out all that is happening right now,' you might say. We have been focusing on the why of the disintegration. Now we are focusing on reconstituting your identity. Even if you hurt someone (non maliciously), the outcome does not determine your goodness."

"Some demands need an honest response like, 'I am fourteen right now and I can't help you.' It usually takes one month for each year that a person has been stuck. For you that is about 30 months. So relax and enjoy the pain."

"You have been unpopular a lot for being honest even before this. Even when the ID change is done, you will still hurt when you are rejected. This is painful evidence that there are true things about you that upset others. You will someday get past that they are upset, but it will still hurt some. You won't become used to being hurt."

"You asking for help and saying you are needy is a discipline right now for you to accurately portray who you are, so you can feel. Later you will know better what satisfies. In the new, you may keep the same foods or change—you may keep some life-giving things or change, add, or drop things."

"God made you a woman of strength and with the beautiful quality of meekness. Being a strong woman is not bad and you will still be strong in the Lord""

For many years, being a strong woman was one of the principle characteristics for which I had rejected myself. What a relief to hear that it was not bad. JW's prayers encouraged me further in the reconstituting phase of my ID crises. Here is another example of how to pray for someone going through an ID change.

"Father God, Surround and help your child to explore her world, your world, herself, even the hostile parts of the world to discover all you are and learn to be fearless. Strengthen her to stand, but as she's doing hard things, be her rest and give her provision and encourage her in little ways. Send some trickles from a lot of places to keep her from being overwhelmed and losing who she is. Thank you for all the parts of her. Be like a parent over a newborn, looking at her fingers and toes, delighting in her."

Another day JW's kind words filled my heart with hope. I told him, 'You always talk so great to me and you have never put me down.' He answered, "One has to be careful how one talks to princesses." I said, 'Yes, Princes do know how to talk to princesses, don't they?' He said, "That is one of the things the King teaches His children."

Knowing I was God's child and a princess was not a new concept, but really feeling it throughout myself was new. I burst into grateful prayer as I realized that God was showing me something about His omnipresence and His timing for my healing: "Jesus, you don't give my love to another. The part of you that is mine is always mine and only mine, even though you have a trillion others. You like me. You brought me out of the black tunnel and said, "You are right on time!"

When someone is going through a deep healing or ID change, it is so helpful to have people around that can say who the person is. They must avoid anyone who might give them toxic accusations. As I learned from JW, I now pray for others in this kind of crises that rejection would be minimal, and I also pray against harassment from the enemy. I pray that the person will not avoid the pain they've been hiding from, but feel it as it comes. I am willing and glad to sit with them while they hurt and not try to fix them.

ON JESUS MEETING ALL OUR NEEDS

For years I had tried to fix and/or avoid the pain in my marriage. One of the mainstays of my journey through the years was to turn to Jesus and remind myself that Jesus meets all my needs. This was important to cling to when my needs were not getting met in my experience. These days I felt a great lack of needs getting met anywhere. JW helped me see that I'd allowed an unbalanced lie to creep into my thinking that had blinded me to the depth of pain that I'd buried inside. JW had a different perspective on Jesus meeting all our needs:

"Some people who teach that Jesus meets all our needs make it a little crooked. In Ephesians 4:7, and 11-12, it says that each one of us has grace given according to the measure of Christ's gift. Then it lists the people God gives to build up the body of Christ. Christ's gift is people. Some of the people do not carry out their responsibilities; therefore, others do not get their needs met. If we don't do our part, some needs won't get met. If Jesus met all needs, there would not be any hungry people in the world. Ultimately He is our all, but since He made us for each other we are to meet some needs. Spouses are supposed to meet each other's needs as well, and when they don't it is very painful."

"Christ needs to heal a legitimate need that was not done for you. He will heal and restore but it did NOT get met. Say it, admit it, and grieve it. Some failed you, some betrayed you, and some deserted you in your moment of biggest need. I know you will forgive and stay open to most of them because that is Barbara-like."

Again, JW encouraged honesty that leads to grieving. Grieving allows healing and restoration. Jesus would heal and fill the emptiness left in the wake of the unmet needs, but it was important for me to admit they were unmet. I needed to admit how painful it was when someone was "supposed" to meet needs and they didn't. This was very reassuring and brought the balance that I needed without taking away from the fact that ultimately Jesus is to be our "all." Like other seeming paradoxes in my Christian walk, I rested in knowing that while Jesus is our all, we need people as well.

ON BEING BARBARA-LIKE

JW often used a phrase that was new to me. For example, if I was taking a negative about something that I should not, he might ask me, "What is like you here? What response is like you?' If I told him about a situation where I loved someone unconditionally, he would tell me, "That is like you," or "That is Barbara-like." Or in other circumstances he might ask, "Are you acting like yourself here?" I began to see the value in using these ideas. It was helping me define "Barbara." I had spent years defining my self in Christ, but was still stumbling around finding out who Barbara is. I was to surround myself with people who would tell me who I am and stay away from those who did not for a while. These phrases help us look at what we are like in different areas. For example, JW often told me, "It is like you to hurt like that when someone misunderstands." "It is like you to be loving and bonding and nurturing." When he said these things, they not only told me who I am, but if I had felt a negative about some of them, it changed the negative to a positive. These things that are Barbara-like could be unique about me or they could be things that are like Jesus and the heart He gave me. Here are some other examples.

"If you are not sure, ask the Holy Spirit who you are in a situation. What is like you here? Is it like you to suffer gladly, or is it like you to walk away from harm?"

"When you feel distress from someone's evaluation of you, ask yourself, 'Is this fitting or not fitting?' If it fits, you will know and gladly repent. If it doesn't ignore it."

This particular issue of sometimes not being comfortable being myself was a long-standing one, as I mentioned in Part One. It was one of the principle things that I worked on after I learned the exchanged life. Often I felt that I got in trouble for being myself. For example in a small group I am not shy about sharing and expressing my views. I am also very honest and open. This can frighten people and make them feel uncomfortable. For years when I felt like I was "just being myself," my husband, and others around me, would get very upset. I continually beat up on myself when it happened. I did not want to offend people; I wanted them to like me. I rejected that part of my personality and tried to be different.

I am an analytical thinker. That can threaten people. It drove my husband crazy for me to shoot a bunch of questions at him about something we were discussing. One day after I did this, he walked out of the house. I was again crying and begging God to change me. I hated myself because Jim got so upset with me. That day God spoke to me and said, "I made you analytical. Stop beating yourself because of his reaction to it." That was a great insight from the Lord and helped me better accept that particular aspect of my personality. I gained some freedom while at the same time asking God to keep me from shooting questions at Jim.

I am a strong woman and not afraid to lead out. That does not go well with many men. Also I like to fix things around the house and Jim did not. But sometimes when I did, he got upset. Or if I wanted to help him, he got upset. In group if I "talked too much," or I was too bluntly honest with someone, I got rejected for being honest. Of course I wanted God to work on anything He wanted to change or modify about me, but I most often took that

I was bad even if I was not. JW had to help me learn that I was not bad for being myself. These are examples of "vanilla" kinds of things that are just me, not bad, unless used harmfully.

"When you are being yourself and someone gets upset, the unspoken message is, 'You're bad for me.' Somewhere along the line after hearing it continuously, you can decide to modify yourself to be less bad. The message you have gotten from many in your community is that the basic 'you' is bad for people generally. <u>This is the most enormous injury a human being can do to another.</u> Even rape would not do so much damage since at least somehow "pleasure' was involved in that.

Being upset with you for being yourself says that when you are yourself you are not 'Bringer of Joy' but 'Bringer of Misery.' Your basic nature is toxic. There is no way to defend or argue—you have bad effects every time. People who do this are saying, 'Anytime I hurt, you are bad. You are bad because I hurt.' These are 'picker powered messages.' *(sark)* We need to be the sparkle in others' eyes."

This jewel about Jesus acting like Himself also helped me accept myself more easily:

"When Jesus went to the Cross he did not say, 'Well, if I just hadn't done that cleansing of the Temple thing, I wouldn't be in this mess---.'"

It seems that JW is saying here that Jesus went to the Cross because it was like Him to do so. He did not blame the people taking Him there and question whether He could have avoided it by being nicer. When He cleansed the temple He was acting like Himself even if it caused flak (rejection that brought the cross.) He acted like Himself no matter what—whether it brought love or rejection. I needed to learn to be myself no matter what, instead of worrying so much about whether I would get in trouble or not. JW told me, "Our biggest stress comes from not being ourselves." I grew to see how true his statement is and how difficult it is to act differently than who I am in order to please someone else.

"You will be a mystery to folks as you learn these things. They will see you as bizarre. You are different—a frustration, the only kid on the block with a motorcycle. You will grieve that they are on their trikes and that they misunderstand, but you won't resist being who you are. If they don't like things you do, you will feel the feelings but not be controlled and pushed into not acting like yourself."

In a conversation where I told JW I had done something unusual but Barbara-like he responded,

"I love it that you danced last night with a new friend. Her showing up should get you good and miserable again—the light casts a long shadow. What would you have felt or been like if she had shown up at fourteen?"

I understood that JW was again saying that when I got loved or cared about it would bring more thawing of the pain that had been buried for so long. It was one of his "tongue-in- cheek" remarks that he is famous for. Light from this friend's love would make the shadow of that pain visible again. If I had had a friend at fourteen that helped me dance and return to joy, I would have been a very different person—one without a trauma. Traumas are not the same when they are dealt with at the time they happen. They get comforted, explained, healed and not buried. This is what is needed when helping children as they grow up—to have no fear of asking for comfort, no fear of being condemned if they mess up, to be able to resolve issues as they happen and not bury them so they are not traumatic.

ON BEING REFINED

A month after finding BOJ, the pain was still very big. God led me through an exercise that was like physically tearing my lost loved ones from my heart. One by one I symbolically pulled them out, literally acting it out with my hand and arm. I pulled out, as well, the possibility of having them in my life, or having them how I wanted them. It was agony. It felt very real in the physical realm, but afterwards it was very healing and relieving. All the rest of the week I felt like I was crazy to still be hurting so much.

I asked JW what was wrong with me. He answered:

"There is nothing wrong with you. That is an insult to God. What is right with you is what hurts. We are at a point where it should hurt like this. There is room to go wrong now if you reject your capacity to hurt like this. Grow through the pain to embracing your capacity to hurt. When your suffering is done you will be 'without sin.' (1 Peter 4:1) When you freely embrace the hurt, you will have nothing to fear or be scared of. Tearing loved ones from His heart would feel the same way to God. To turn away would be wrong. If you reach the highest level saturated with pain, embrace and hold on to it, not just to the pain, but to yourself—to yourself who can hurt that way. God is perfecting you—a person of deep value. If you didn't hurt or weren't bothered, you wouldn't be the person you are. Bring every bit of the hurt in, don't miss a part."

"You may have to hide some of the hurt from certain people, like children or others that cannot bear it. That is different than rejecting or denying the pain. Even God hides things. The strength of the relationship and maturity levels determine what we hide or don't. He debated about hiding from Abraham about Sodom and Gomorrah. (Genesis 18:17, 2 Chronicles 20:7, Isaiah 41:8, James 2:23)

And another prayer from JW:

"Lord God, Speak the truth to her about the pain. Show her how every time you send her another opportunity to hurt, that you are doing a great thing to show Barbara her value. You are making her new and restoring her. Show her some things of joy today."

'Is this because of what Jesus did on the Cross, like that?' I asked.

"Yes, it is," JW answered softy. "Only something good and holy would hurt like this. Your capacity to love has to be equal to your hurt. You love greatly or you wouldn't hurt like this. It is proof of who you are and how full of love you are. It is in every part of you— your body, your soul, your emotions. It is a purifying process in you and all that will be left is love. It will sound like nonsense if you try to share it with others. If God hadn't sustained you, you would not be here." (Hebrews 2:10, 5:8, 4:11) (*Isaiah* 41:9b)

What a privilege to take His yoke and learn of Him—to take up the lack in the afflictions of Christ—to know how full of love I am because I knew how much I hurt. The vessel was being shaped for the Master's use.

Knowing that God would use me for deeply loving His people made me want to shout! My love for Him was growing by leaps and bounds. This was the ultimate experience and relationship with Him. I thanked Him for the rape. It was part of my history that He could heal and use for others. I felt so important and valuable. Scriptures came newly alive each day as I spent time alone there in my room.

ON VALUE

Not only did I learn that the amount of pain I was going through equaled the amount of love that was in me, I also learned that it was a measure of my value. All I had to do to keep this in mind was to look at Jesus' pain on the cross (not just the physical) and know how valuable He is. These are the jewels on value:

"Great value is in you, because when you are injured you feel pain. When evil (injury) collides with value it equals pain. The greater the capacity to feel the pain reveals the greater value. If evil finds evil it has no problem and there is no pain."

"Embrace the parts that hurt because of their value: toe parts, bonding parts, unity parts, mercy parts, etc."

"When you see the part that is hurting, you can find one of your characteristics. For example—you are hurting because someone is disloyal—your loyalty is hurting. If you are hurting because you are honest, your honesty is hurting. This will help you name your characteristics like loyalty and honesty."

After hearing this I asked JW, 'Aren't all people valuable?' The jewel was:

"Yes, all people are valuable, but if they are not feeling their pain then they have no *awareness* of their value. They are trying to maintain their value without really being aware of it."

"There is a deeper thing here about value: God sent His Son to suffer for us and that shows our value to God, right? Then it says God sent many sons to suffer in order to complete the sufferings of Christ. (Colossians 1:24) The point is, if God let his daughter get raped, be deserted, die, suffer—she is of incredible value. The only difference in your suffering and Christ's is that yours can't atone for sin. You are bringing the same message to His world as Christ did. Every ingrown toenail that Jesus had, every thumb hit with a hammer were all suffering. Paul's shipwrecks and beatings—they were suffering. It's like God is saying, 'It is worth so much to others that I would let my daughter suffer to show her she is my stand-in for Christ.' The amount of suffering indicates the amount of value." (Hosea 6:1, 3, 6)

"Most people conclude that their suffering means that they *don't* have value. They think towards God, 'If I mattered, you wouldn't make me suffer.' They don't appreciate others' value either."

"You are grieving because you know the ones who are hurting you are valuable, too. You suffer because they are valuable, wishing that they could know their value better."

I asked, 'Because I have healing and understand more, does this mean I have to go back home right now?' "No, you have choices: you can appeal to Caesar or be let down in a basket over the wall. Don't go back to be mistreated. You're valuable. Find Barbara-like ways to say, 'I'm valuable.'"

"We only hurt/pain/grieve over valuable things. There is no sorrow over garbage or discards."

ANOTHER FRIEND'S INTERCESSION--THE TURNING POINT

As my grieving continued, one day my friend Wanda came to visit. She had been helping me off and on and had been with me one of the times I expressed my rage out loud. She is a great prayer warrior and at this visit she prayed spiritual warfare for me, telling me the vision that she was getting. "There is a deep hole inside you and it is a pit of darkness with a ladder going down inside. There are black, heavy boots on the ladder. The enemy has been using this pit. Now I see the light of the Holy Spirit coming like a laser beam, filling the hole from the bottom up, dispelling the darkness and sealing the hole. I see blackness going out of your hand. The enemy stole your whole life. It was more than a broken heart; it was a mortal wound. You are so valuable that the enemy went after you when you were very young. He took your dignity and stripped you of everything that gave you any reason to live. He meant it for destruction but God was not surprised and brought it to greatness."

Wanda said that Satan had me in his grasp through a spirit of Jezebel whose worst enemies are prophets. "That spirit hates prophets and their words of repentance. It does not like your outspokenness. That spirit's goal is to block repentance. It is a spirit of manipulation and intimidation that leads to domination," she told me. "You are under its hold, dominated by others' evaluations of you." As she prayed and shared, I knew God set me free from that pull. She told me, "Be willing, at all cost, to no longer relinquish the God-given right to be who you are. Take back what God gave you-- your dignity and your esteem. Your very life was violated. All the prophets I have known are very lonely and misunderstood because they go straight to the heart of things and people can't take that. Take your life back." There are not words for how much better I felt after this session of prayer.

This time with Wanda was right before Easter. The blackness was gone from inside and joy was in its place. On Good Friday, 1995, I wrote a poem in my journal, celebrating what a different Easter this was!

Joy Comes

Long I waited for Your touch,
The Great Physician holds the knife.
Knowing only You could do here
What needed doing in my life.

My name You gave me two years ago.
I grasped it by the hand to find.
It didn't always fit the scene
Until total healing in your time.

Yesterday you closed the wound
And glory came within the dark.
Your laser beam cut through with Light
Cleansing, closing every part.

Dr. Jim his prayer so strong
Asked to see the joy burst through.
The name confirmed and spoken now

Bubbled and bounced as she was new.

Resurrection comes from You alone
Only comes when old life is dead.
Down to zero I finally came,
"How long, O Lord?" was all I said.

Joy has filled my heart today.
Resurrection with my Lord.
Take the joy and love inside
And spread them all around my world.

Dear Lord, this Joy I bring to you
Bursting forth out of the grave,
I take the name and wait on You
To show it 'round, Your love they crave.

After so many months of depression and even thoughts of suicide, with the encouragement of JW and other, I began to truly choose Life again, to declare that I wanted to live and be really alive. I stood up inside against the enemy, or any one else trying to drain life out of me or trying to take it from me by accusations or condemnation.

When I talked next to JW, I asked him if healing the mortal wound would cause me to avoid pain again. Since the pain was diminishing, I wanted to be sure that I would not go backwards. He said:

"No, it won't. But there are two ways you can test to see if you are avoiding pain. You can ask yourself: 'Am I telling the truth about pain? Am I rejecting the parts that hurt?' If you're not doing this then you are okay. The feelings will not return with quite the magnitude. Stand in the healing, not against the feelings."

ON EXPECTING THE WORST

Even though healing the mortal wound had brought relief, I found myself sometimes expecting the worst to happen. I had in the past thought of myself as optimistic. What was different now? JW had a jewel for this:

"Expecting the worst is a standard defense against disappointment. You prepare yourself for the worst because you feel that you can't handle it or you won't have any comfort. Be willing to feel the feelings of disappointment and trade having defenses for something better that God might give in trade. This could be anything good from Him, like closeness to Him, or comfort from an unknown source."

ON KNOWING WHO I AM

After I had been Joann's for about two months, Margaret was able to begin spending time with me again. It was so wonderful to have the love and some comfort again. She was very helpful whenever she could be, as I continued to learn. She helped tell me who I was by calling me gentle and tender. Joann said I am honest and open and positive. Brenda, another helpful friend, told me that the things she most admires about me are how I love so unconditionally and how forgiving I am. JW said it is like me to care what everyone thinks. He does that so easily— he just affirms--when the same things would sound condemning from others.

"You get described only half way by some of your family and friends. But then you need them to enjoy you after they describe you. Part of you is crippled because you were not enjoyed by some people who were supposed to enjoy you. When you let yourself loose inside to be yourself, some did not enjoy you. It is like you to want to be enjoyed. Are all your quirks enjoyable? Not necessarily, but you can be enjoyed after they are described. You need someone to say you're enjoyable. There must be something wrong with JW, the one who is cracked because he enjoys you. And Jesus—well, He enjoys you, too."

One conversation I had with JW was about people accusing me that I was always trying to take over. JW's jewel was about guava fruit this time.

"Do you know what a guava fruit is? It has a very thin skin. It is a picture of someone who does not have a very big 'us zone.' They did not grow up with 'usness' or lots of sharing and togetherness. You do have a very big 'us zone.' Most do not. They live out, 'It's either you or me, babe.' No 'us zone.' Whether you say *me, or you say us,* to you it means 'all is us'. If the other person has a small or no 'us zone' they interpret you through their grid and believe, 'Look at that huge 'me zone,' she's trying to take over.' You say, 'No, it's not really me, it's us. There is no dominance here'. This is your view of the world."

I said to JW, 'Then that's why I'm a good mother—I see the child's world through his or her eyes.' He said:

"Yes, and also a good counselor. Those with a small '*us zone*' will appreciate that you will take care of '*us*' only until they see a huge '*me*.' People with small '*us zones*' have had parents who were narcissistic or with a small '*us zone*' themselves. Narcissists have hardly any '*us zone*' with a huge '*me zone*.' You can be mistaken for narcissism by small '*us zones*' just because you are confident and reach out. The ones with small zones have to develop past the child stage to the adult stage in order to operate more '*us*.' This is one of the reasons you say that you and your siblings 'talk and listen at the same time.' There was a lot of *usness* around your house growing up. The ones with small '*us zones*' see you as very interrupting."

These are examples of the many ways I received help by surrounding myself with those who will say who I am. Many of the accusations and condemnations I heard and took were washed away by JW's truth and catchy ways of describing it. But I did not take his example about being seen as interrupting as an excuse to interrupt. I continued to work very hard on learning to listen more and not interrupt. I mostly talk and listen at the same time with my two sisters and my kids.

As negative situations with friends and loved ones continued, I talked to JW about how I seemed to hope and expect things to change. His jewel describing me there:

"You feel stupid because you keep on being hopeful about someone? You can't help that you hope, that you have a heart like that, that hopes anyway. It is like you to hope. It hurts. Sometimes you wish you didn't care, so it wouldn't hurt."

More on who I am:

"We mustn't let our *sark (flesh)* or anyone else's tell us we are bad—or tell us we are good for that matter, since we can't trust the sark. It is very pleasing to God that I don't allow others to tell me I am bad. You went faster than I did in learning all this," said JW. 'Well, that is because I had a wonderful master to lead me through,' I returned.

"If you name your main characteristic, you will know a lot about yourself. Also what do you get in trouble a lot for? Satan wants to attack you there so you won't live it out. What are the things you won't give up on no matter how big the pain or trouble it brings?"

On this I believe that my main characteristics are honesty, openness and loving unconditionally. It was for sure that Satan had always managed to get me attacked there. Most times I kept on being that way (especially the honesty and loving part) even though I did get in trouble for it. Sometimes I caved in and hid it.

"Satan always acts Satan-like, so God just uses Him when He needs that kind of thing, and redeems it, and Satan is full of rage. If the Old Red Dragon is around, he's bringing a message from God."

"I remind you again the incredible value of having your kind of heart—the kind that loves so unreservedly."

"Continue looking for the treasures here about yourself."

ON SETTLING BEING GOOD AND BAD

In order to understand this next phase of my healing better, I want to explain the principle method that I use when counseling. It is a form of prayer, whereby the hurting person is taken to the place that needs to be healed inside and allowing Jesus to come into the situation to show truth about it and for Him to bring the healing needed. It is like a visual or picture inside, but the Holy Spirit directs and does it. JW and Chuck Kraft had helped me refine this method and I had been using it with the women I counseled. Sometimes Margaret helped me by using this kind of prayer. (See *Deep Wounds, Deep Healing* by Dr. Charles Kraft for a detailed description of this kind of prayer ministry.)

Earlier, JW had encouraged me to quit thinking I had to be so "good." Now it was time to deal with my internal messages and feelings that say, "You are a bad girl." These feelings came from messages that I heard both internally and externally: "You were part of the rape." "You are upset, so stay away from me." "You are mean." "You hurt me." "You are too needy." "You want to be loved."

These feelings were coming from other hurting and closed off parts inside that I decided to call by a kind of descriptive name, like I had BOJ. This part we called "bad girl." JW's responses were specific:

"Feeling like you are a bad girl is a hard feeling to feel. You know you are doing God things, and this feeling of being bad comes up when you get accusations from others. They have very interesting 'glasses' by the way, from some of the things they are calling you. You have not been loved, and what happened when you felt loved by Margaret? You got rejected when you opened up to it, and you got accusations. Some are calling you bad. Now you must look at and talk about how it feels to be a bad girl. You must have felt that way a long time. Embrace that part. Love her. What happened when you got raped? You wanted to be loved, accepted and comforted and you weren't, so you decided you were bad. 'Bad girl' carries that pain of wanting to be loved by people who don't love her. That is a God-like thing. He wants to be loved by people who don't love Him. Allow yourself to feel the pain and in your heart and mind embrace the bad girl parts until they are healed. Let there be no self-rejection that says you are bad for wanting to be loved or that it was your fault you got raped."

After this talk with JW, Margaret was able to take me in prayer to Jesus. Inside like a picture in my mind I saw Jesus, JW and Margaret walking up to 'bad girl' who was standing alone in a desolate place. I told 'bad girl' that I loved her and I asked her to forgive me for thinking she was bad. I then forgave some people who had contributed to me thinking I was bad by their rejection and accusations. We asked 'bad girl' what she needed most. But before she could answer, I knew—she needs to be held! She was the one screaming, "I just want to be held." It was not only BOJ that had screamed that, it was also the part of me who felt she was a bad girl from the rape and the events following.

The black curtain covering Bringer Of Joy when I first found her was a symbol for "bad girl." God had removed the blackness when I was with Wanda, but I had not faced "bad girl." Now more was all falling into place—Bringer of Joy was wounded at the rape and 'bad girl' was the darkness over BOJ from believing she was bad. Margaret ended the prayer session, saying that inside, she, Jesus and JW would take turns holding 'not bad girl' until she was comforted, loved and peaceful. I was so relieved at this release and peace washed over me.

Because I believe that this concept of resolving good and bad that we have to go through is difficult to describe and understand, I would like to quote from *The Red Dragon Cast Down* to help explain it more clearly:

"For an identity to be to be solid, it is more important that it be accurate, rather than either pleasant, nice or positive. We all sense things about ourselves that are painful, shameful or bad, but many parents try to build self-esteem and save their children from pain by telling them nothing but good things about themselves. Equally deadly is the trap of acknowledging the bad but forgetting the child's value. Humanists say as a rule that all bad is imposed from outside, inside the self is good. Christians believe that self has evil in it, but beyond that opinions vary greatly. Whatever else may be meant by sin, it refers to not acting out of our true selves—the selves we were created to be. Sin means it is now possible for us to both act like ourselves and not act like ourselves. We can receive and give life or destroy it. Original sin means it is inevitable that we will fail to act like our true selves because we will be like our parents. The result of neglecting either the evil or the value within a child is that he or she will develop an identity that cannot accommodate both. Either way his identity will not fit what the child knows to be true. The truth is, he is both good and bad, and he will become vulnerable to the first person to recognize this truth in his soul and do something about it." * Paraphrased Pages 83,84

"We must come to terms with both the good and bad within us. Denying the evil in us makes us deny our value. We need identities that include both. Yes, we are loved and we are bad. The God who loves us sees the evil in us, and is prepared to transform death into life." * Paraphrased Page 239

ON PARENTING AGAIN

Although my four children were grown by this time, I loved the things that JW told me about parenting. They work well with my wonderful grandchildren, and these jewels usually apply to re-parenting (spiritual adoption) as well.

"Each of us is born with a self that is too small, but this evil cannot be corrected by anything we do. We cannot raise a child with a good enough self, even by following Scriptural principles. We fool ourselves when we think we can rear or train our children in such a way as to eliminate or even reduce this problem. What is missing is the life we cannot give that comes from the new heart that Jesus gives." * Paraphrased Pages 238, 239 *The Red Dragon.*

"All children are to be taught that God esteems them and this value is truly part of them. They are to learn of their great value, which does not come from their own actions. We possess this value even when we are dead (Spiritually) (Romans 5:8). Another way to say this is that our value never comes from our goodness. It is clear to me that failing to build strong identities in children leaves them open to anyone who wants to tell them who they are." * Paraphrased Page 238 *The Red Dragon*

"Confessing the good and bad in and around us summarizes a process that leads us towards God, the only hope of our decontamination." * *Page 168 The Red Dragon*

"No child can tolerate being a parent's life line."

"Kids take care of parents out of fear that the parent won't be ok. Then the child can't feel dependent like they should."

"A good parent is always ready to move close even while the child experiences the negative, even if that negative is about the parent."

"If a child is not left too long in a negative feeling, then he can learn to feel all feelings because he will return to joy from them. This task is accomplished by 18 months."

"A baby that has several good, loving bonds is jealousy-proofed."

"Good parents know that their greatest satisfaction comes from serving, protecting, and enjoying the child who now receives life from them." If parents don't protect, serve and enjoy, it makes a brokenhearted child." * Page 82 *The Red Dragon*

"We should not protect our children from all discomfort or mistakes. The proper method of self-repair is to learn to ask for and receive what we need while simultaneously developing strength to handle the pain of waiting." * Page 81 *The Red Dragon*

"By the age of three an infant knows his/her feelings and how to ask for needs to be met. There have been strong loving and caring bonds with a mother who builds into the child. She guesses and teaches him to know his needs and ask. The better she is at guessing the better the child grows."

"Father bonds affect children's views of God. Weak father bonds are most often caused by absent or ineffectual fathers. This tends to produce one of two effects: deep hostility or idealization from their children. God, like all fathers can survive anger and hostility far better than idealization. If examined closely, God will fail abysmally to reach our ideals. He is clearly not the ideal, protective, nice father of our dreams. He is not fair and introduces such unfair concepts as mercy, grace and forgiveness. He is notorious for his absences and silence." * Paraphrased from Pages 157-158 *The Red Dragon*

"The other type father bond that affects the view of God is when fathers are angry and/or dangerous. They have this feature in common: neither will accept problems as their own responsibility. The result of a father who blames, shames and rejects is that his children take "badness" as their identity. An inconsistent father who goes from good father to bad father causes a battle that will be won by whichever side is stronger. If the father tries to be good but fails to be consistent, the child emotionally concludes that evil is stronger than good." * Paraphrased Page 160 *The Red Dragon*

"A person who is terrified of God cannot just go directly to Him with their burdens and pain. It does not work, because fear bonds can never return us to joy (that is: someone is glad to be with me)." * Paraphrased Page 216 *The Red Dragon*

"Love has only the credibility it earns through suffering (John 10:18). Strong love bonds with one's father reveal a parent eager to share the good and bad of life with his child. Joy is this dad's standard and the return to joy his goal. These bonds do not break due to pain or fear. He demonstrates love through availability and interest in his child's identity whether he is there at the moment or not. Healthy love bonds grow stronger both by sharing positive and negative emotion, and by getting closer and moving apart. They help everyone feel stable and act like himself or herself. They provide both freedom and connection." * Paraphrased Page 162 *The Red Dragon*

"Tests of faith are not for children. Isaac, Ishmael, and Mary had well developed selves before their callings. When Abraham and Isaac went up the mountain, God demonstrated three things crucial to child rearing. First, God revealed Abraham's character to Isaac. Abraham was a killer, carrying fire and a knife in his hand. Faith does not make us less deadly. True people of faith must eventually show their children the knife. We must admit we can kill but we cannot give life. Second, God showed Isaac he was not a suitable sacrifice for redemption. All children of faith are also killers and unfit sacrifices. Third, God became the One who provided. God alone was able to give life and find a suitable sacrifice. My point is that Abraham was not the destroyer of Isaac's identity while his son was growing a self. He did not rear Isaac with a knife hung over his cradle. He raised his son to be strong, mature, and thoughtful—and only then did they go to the mountain. Only when they gave their best could it be proven insufficient. We bring our children up to be their very best and then when we are called to go up the mountain we can say, 'My very best will destroy you. God will give life. I cannot decontaminate you from your killing nature or even myself. Only God can save us now.' This sanctifying process of redemption will shake our identities and the whole structure of our communities." * Paraphrased Pages 249, 250 *The Red Dragon*

"Only those who have received life can give life because we are dependent creatures. We are dependent for every breath. We cannot manufacture life."

PART FOUR

THE END AND THE BEGINNING

ON PAIN OF DIVORCE WHILE ADJUSTING THE NEW IDENTITY

The biggest fear I dreaded came true on September 29, 1995 when Jim called and asked for a divorce. This was not what my dream had been at eighteen when I married and "dedicated my life to be a Christian wife and mother." This was not what I wanted to happen. This did not line up with my ideas of walking with God. This did not line up with our grown children's expectations of the way our family would be "until death did us part." It was a nightmare and I ached to make others, especially the children, more comfortable with this. But it was another big mess that I could not fix.

In June, Joann had told me she wanted to be alone in her apartment again so I moved into an apartment of my own. Because I still hoped that I'd be able to return home, I took a six months' lease. But before the six months ended, Jim called with his news. In December when my lease expired, I moved in with Margaret and her two teens. She and her teens had some serious wounds and issues of their own. This only complicated my mess more because, even though I was technically "the counselor," and the "adoptive mother," I was emotionally raw, but I did tried to help any way I could.

I loved Margaret and her kids deeply and I was very committed to them even though most people did not understand the Spiritual adoption. Because of my neediness and their damage, we vacillated between best friends and best enemies. There were so many parallel conflicts and problems to my marriage that it was difficult to know if the pain was past or present. Whenever I blew it and hurt Margaret or her family, I still hated myself and hurt very much because of it.

JW encouraged me to find someone else with whom to do my processing, but most of the others who had helped me months before were busy and hard to get together with. It felt like I did not belong anywhere again. I had to turn to God moment by moment for comfort and not look to Margaret for any help.

My pain grew tremendously again as I struggled to walk out the jewels that I had been learning. I had to process the pain of my broken marriage and try to continue helping Margaret and her family while I was such a mess myself. These are some of the jewels that JW put into my storm-tossed, battered treasure chest while I worked through the divorce and the adjustments of a new life and identity.

"What will it take for you to be 100% at peace about the divorce?" he asked.

"To know from God what to do," was my first answer. This was very difficult for me to know because I saw the pain that our oldest son, Jim, was feeling. It was harder for him to understand, I think, partly because he had been gone from home longer than the other children. He also was upset with me because issues from his childhood came up during this time. I wanted to remain open and patient with him so that he could work through whatever he needed to do. I told all my children long before this that I wanted them to tell me anything I had done to hurt them growing up and allow me to ask forgiveness.

JW encouraged me—"A mother wants to show her son what God has for him here. She wishes she could save her son from pain, but she has been learning not to avoid pain. You must share the pain. Teach him about pain. Find elders in the community to help him if he has none. Part of your pain is from wanting to reach a son and help him know where God is, and you can't explain or predict what is happening. No one can answer all the questions here."

I was not able to help my son as I wanted to and I felt very sad. Eventually we were able to talk and have our relationship back, but until he was ready there was not much I could do except love him and pray for him.

All of us were floundering under the weight of the divorce. There was no precedence for how to act, what to think, what to say. JW reminded me

"When someone does something that your mind has nowhere to put it (like ask for a divorce), it shakes your sense of reality; it is unthinkable and so unpredictable. It rocks your sense of judgment and you doubt your own ability to judge. It would be like someone telling you that I (JW) have been running a white slavery ring. You would have no place to even process it."

"You have never been asked for a divorce before. What is like Barbara here? Do you sit and wait or run towards everyone's rules that say 'No divorce.' What little help those rules are! Even the best of Evangelical Christians head towards legalism as if there were some way the Law could save us now. Christ arrived to reveal truth, not make things look right. Remember our talks about the sark and its inability to discern truth and 'the right thing.' You cannot just try to look right. You must listen to God. You will betray yourself if you just go and try to get 'elders' on your side and/or to say you're ok and be ok for your son. Jesus knows how much it hurts to be misunderstood."

"I have the sense that you could get lost easier if you listen to others' comments like, 'Barbara will be ok because she always does the right thing.' Remember you are a daughter of God who cares for your children. You will get your focus clear and know what a mother is to do. What will a mother teach about pain? They need to know about pain. They will learn from you and/or by watching you."

There *was* fear in me that I would do something wrong here. Deep questions arose: Was I truly free to follow God's leading no matter what? What are my opinions on divorce? What am I going to do with all this? I vividly remember one day, on a Sunday, before Jim's call, I took the whole day to get away and pray. I went to a park with my Bible and journal. I told God that all I'd ever wanted was what He wants in my life. I told Him I would go back home if He said to. The only sense I got all day was that I was not to go back. I couldn't even tell people that I had that leading. It sounded heretical and crazy. JW talked me through it:

"You must let the world know your opinions. That does not mean you are going along with divorce, even if you divorce. What sort of person is Barbara? She does have opinions about divorce and fairness. If you hide the opinions, you are going along in a passive way. Don't make it easy for your husband to ignore who you are. This whole year has been about your identity. Will he be married to Barbara or to the fantasy that he wished her to be? It is very important to continue stating who you are, even if it is ignored. If someone does not want to take responsibility for their stomping you, you must limit additional beatings. If they are not willing to suffer through their own pain and see their part, there will be no resolution."

JW shared a little about his journey that is described in *The Red Dragon*. "When my heart broke during my own mess and I had no support, Kitty (his wife) said, 'You can't quit now, you have to fix the mess you have made of our lives.' I was too broken to fix it even if I wanted to. God worked in Kitty's heart and she 'put down her gun.' She worked on her part and we found resolution."

"When one gets lots of blaming by others, one can get the impression that he or she deserves all the pain and anger sent their way."

"Even God is not bound by a 'no coming and going' clause. Jesus did come and go and the disciples got upset. Your pain has been, 'All my life I've not been seen as who I am and I've fought to be what others wanted instead."

I said again, 'NO MORE!'

Months later, I found myself quite a recluse, not wanting to go out very often. I asked JW about this.

"You have taken such a different path than your community. Not only are you divorcing, in addition you are living with another family that needs help. People do not understand Spiritual adoption. They don't understand how you can try to help this family. Spiritual adoption scares people and that fear creates distance instead of closeness.

You feel sad and abandoned again, like there is a glass there that you can see through, but you don't know where you are any more. It takes 'pretending' to be with people who do not understand and that is too much effort right now, especially when they don't act like what you are going through is important."

"You still need someone to be on your side with your feelings and join you so you won't feel so alone. You were not believed about your reasons for separating from your husband and that area is still beaten up. You must get in touch with that pain of not being believed. That is a very hurtful thing. It is very important to be believed, especially in a deep and vulnerable time. Find some more people who will believe you and understand. Pray for more people to help you."

I did pray for more help, but the help remained scarce and infrequent.

Negotiations about divorce can get very sticky and mine were no different. At one point I felt odd talking to Jesus about it all. How could I be okay with breaking my promises and be going against His teachings. I felt like He must be frowning at me and I felt odd that He could love us both and both of us talk to Him and be hurt. JW used an illustration about Solomon's temple being destroyed:

"The Babylonians came and destroyed the temple of God. It is amazing that God would let it be destroyed and the people carried off. You have tried to keep things together and now have amazement that it was wrecked. You thought He built it and you worked on it. This can't be okay. You can't just watch and say, 'Oh this is fine by me.' God grieves, you grieve, all grieve. It somehow turns into a frown from Jesus because when <u>you</u> have frowned on some people, it made a mess and you had to clean it up."

"There is a theme here. When you are a disappointing person to others or to yourself, as you are or have been through this, you aren't able to get close and be welcomed. You are rejected and they just get mad. It is not an all right place to be. You are left isolated and criticized. The normal response for disappointment should be, 'I am disappointed in what you did. So come here and sit on my knee so we can be disappointed together and return to joy. There is a lack of modeling about sitting on the knee."

That was an understatement. I could not imagine a response like sitting on the knee and being talked with instead of pushed away.

"Whatever place that you bond with someone is the place that will be easily affected. Whatever things are most important to you is where the other will have the most impact. If you bond right over a wound, a hurt place, the other person will have free rein there to easily affect that place. They have a choice of helping you there or stomping on the wound. This makes us very vulnerable."

It seemed to me that JW was saying that my marriage was very important to me. I was disappointing everyone and they were stomping on the wounds of my failure. I was vulnerable to their evaluations and open to stomps. I longed for some knee-sitting help.

And, adding to the whirlwind, JW pointed out, I still carried elements of thinking that my love could change things, both with my marriage and Margaret and her family.

"Your love can only show up what is really there and how ugly things are if that is what is really there. You don't stop loving, though. And even when you don't stop, it doesn't change the situation. You are still being refined to bring you to say the truth here like Jesus did, 'Lazarus is dead and he stinketh.' You wish instead that the truth could be 'If only I'd had more love' or "if only I could make everything okay." Or like Mary and Martha, 'If You had only been here....'"

"Isn't it sad," JW asked, "that love won't get everyone well?" "Yes," I responded, "there would be many well." He responded, "Love by itself is not sufficient. There has to be willingness to face the pain along with the love."

I responded aloud to Jesus, "This is a parallel to You, Lord. Your absolute love was not enough to get everyone to know You, nor was the Father's love enough. You had to go through the pain so we *could* all be well, but all don't receive it." JW agreed how it really hurts when you've poured your life into someone and you watch them flush it. *What pain the Father must have to watch this world*, I thought.

"You have to understand the results of love. Love brings out what is really inside others—maybe darkness. God loved Hitler. Should you anticipate that you will have better results than God with your love? There are choice-points with the person receiving the love. When the inside comes out, they have an element of choice of which direction to go—deal with it, deny it or ignore it. When we quit expecting words or love to work, then we don't get louder or more emotional."

"You can touch up a wrecked car here and there, but it doesn't change that it hit a brick wall."

It took me a long time and a lot of conversations with God and JW to learn and walk out the new things they had been telling me. Rejection and accusations still hurt. JW continued to say things about acting like myself:

"You have to be like a pine tree—no matter the wind that comes, you are a pine tree. When you are down you need a mirror to tell you who you are. Sometimes you do not get the true mirroring. Some will never understand, appreciate, care or edify. They will be very annoyed by you being you. That does not make you less important. You can choose to be yourself anyway." Then he asked, "Does it still hurt you that some don't like you?"

I answered, 'Yes, and I tell myself that it is like me to hurt like this, and I hurt.'"

One day when I talked to JW I told him I'd had a good day. He said laughingly, "You mean someone missed a chance at getting mad at you?"

I answered, 'Yeah, it's the norm to have someone mad at me, but God and you love me. Y'all even *like* me and are good mirrors for me. It feels so good to know that you and God know I'm not perfect and still love me. And now I know it better and I don't have to fret.'

For the next few days the grief returned over the loss of my friend Jenny, my husband and all the other friends that were lost to me. I had horrible dreams and a lot of anger. I had to write and draw in my journal to get out the anger because it was too big and emotional to say out loud without proper comfort and safety. It was like cancer and I wanted it out. It came from different places in my life.

Processing continued three steps forward and two back again. The good and bad dilemma returned, as once again accusations tossed me up and down. I even gave up on God at one point. JW said:

"You are hanging over a well. You are feeling unknown and not understood again. You are not saying, 'Gee, I'm sorry they don't see me and understand me.' You're getting in the 'bad girl' state and falling into the well. Let's go a step lower than the well. Do your feelings convince you that you are bad? When you are a nicely functioning adult, they do not. When you are exhausted, they can. When your identity is solid it doesn't fall apart if feelings are big. When it does collapse you could say, 'Here I am, feeling all bad, but I am ok and this pain shows my worth.' But you are trying to keep the identity strong by your thoughts instead of letting yourself feel bad and still say you are worthwhile. We can't think our way out of things.

There is progress as you are getting more disconnected from the old fear of outcomes. God is cementing: 'Just because there is a negative outcome does not mean I am bad.' Giving up on God this week was good. When you have lost all hope you can know anything, even God, and cannot determine if you are good or bad or anything else, then that puts Him in charge of your good and the figuring out."

"You will not lose the ground you have gained in your healing, even when it appears you have not had a healing."

ON THINGS NOT WORKING

It was now June 1996. The divorce was final and Jim called to tell me he was going to remarry. I told him all I ever had wanted was for him to be happy and I hoped he would be. The day he called I was moving from Margaret's apartment into my own house with her and her teens, plus one of their friends, another troubled teen. That adjustment was very frustrating on top of everything else. Nothing seemed to go right anywhere. Anger flew around the house like a flock of crows. I struggled constantly with rage at my frustrating housemates. Some days I felt that God was not listening to my cries and other days I was screaming out my pain alone with Him. JW had to help me see my frustrations were from feelings of powerlessness. I had little control over the teens in my house, their activities were stepping on my boundaries and I was carrying a physical and financial load that was overwhelming. I had forgotten many of my jewels, thinking that things shouldn't hurt and things should work out with all these new situations. The marriage was over, but now the problems came with new adjustments with housemates.

"You are moving towards understanding, 'this hurts and it doesn't work'. You are called to continue being who you are even, and when, this hurts and it doesn't work. Love is constant no matter if it hurts and doesn't work. Stay connected. God stayed connected even when apart from His Son. What do you do with the pain? David did not eat while his child was ill. After he died, David ate. (Samuel 12:15-23) There was nothing he could do to change things. When you are able to accept that you can't make things work, then peace and joy will come."

JW reminded me often how difficult it is to remember who I am when tired or overwhelmed:

"When you get tired or over the level you can endure, you 'lose it' emotionally and hurt those you don't want to hurt. You forget who you are. Discover what is like you when over your endurance level. This will help you not do something that is really not like who you are. For example, you do not wish to hurt with your words. It is more like you to disengage, go away and calm yourself, then return. Or it is like you to remember that 'words don't help.' And you can let Jesus be your patience."

"I have been waiting for you to truly know that neither love nor words will make things work with some people. You have to understand that love brings out what is inside and that is not always pleasant."

Living with my housemates kept my stomach in a knot. Accusations came frequently as I tried desperately to achieve some kind of order in our household. Like most teens, these didn't like any kind of rules—house or otherwise.

"Everyone, your family and friends and your new housemates, is looking at you for it to turn out right. 'You should know,' they think. Everyone, especially the housemates, is saying, 'Because it hurts, you are hurting us.' You have not been very successful this year in making things turn out right.

Remember the sark with its severely messed up judgment mechanism? Remember it always judges wrongly and tries to make us think we can know what is good and bad. It says something like, 'If it doesn't work you were wrong; if they hurt, I am bad'. As long as we go by our *sark,* which never judges rightly, things will always be hurting and not working. You are moving beyond that to life in the Spirit. You will not be able to prove anything to any of them though. Part of being free is that your stomach is not hostage to it turning out okay and the knots you get will stop.

I knew that household order was part of healthy living. I'd already reared four children to adulthood. But there was not much I could say that did not bring forth some kind of wrath as I tried to deal with "handicapped" children. JW responded to their accusations of having to walk on eggshells.

. 'Walking on eggshells' is a metaphor for, 'I can make it turn out right or okay.' When one of your housemates accusingly says that they have to walk on eggshells with you, they are saying either they or you can, or have to, make it turn out right. Keep being who you are and trusting Jesus. It has not been very long that you have been out of the disintegration and there are many painful things going on in your life at the same time. When the pain gets this big it is called 'accelerated pain' because it is coming from so many different directions."

"Look at the pain in your life and see where evil impacts the things God put in your heart, like loving, bonding and nurturing, wanting to help people. In the past the enemy lined up against what God meant to be and made it hurt so much you wouldn't try it again—you would stop being you. You are learning this is not the way to walk"

"When you encounter hostility, keep affirming that you are not a nasty person. You are stronger inside but your body is not yet. You can handle the *thought* of getting shot, but your body cannot take it and probably never will."

As I tried day after day to maintain some balance of sanity with all that was going on, there was more negative than positive around our house. If I said anything about boundaries or gave reminders about house rules, I was instantly accused of being bad. JW had to tell me over and over how to walk in this new mess I was in.

"When you are expressing feelings and the housemates hear that you want them to change, that is their dysfunction. There is a difference between saying that you feel something and giving some kind of request for changes. In their dysfunction and discomfort, they hear, 'I have to change' or, 'You have to not make me feel this way anymore.' In order for you to express feelings they will have to separate feelings from changes, but they may not be able to do this. Feelings are just feelings. For them you are pulling on their past pain. If you are discussing change, you will use different words and you will make it clear."

ON IMMATURE THINKING

Many of my conversations with JW helped me live more peacefully with my housemates, as well as relating better in general, as I better understood immaturity and the way people's growth fits into the maturity levels. When relating to people who have infant or child level maturity, it is helpful to understand how they think. These jewels were scattered throughout my time with JW.

"If someone believes, 'If you love me you will protect me from pain,' then if you hurt them, it means you don't love them. This is a misunderstanding of pain and love."

"I repeatedly forget that what I say is inconsequential. When someone is immature, their feelings align their thoughts. Maturity uses thoughts to align feelings. Sometimes you still believe an explanation (your words) will change the person. They don't care what you say, they just realign with the feelings and transfer the words to what <u>they</u> feel. They do not sort truth and untruth then realign the feelings and behavior. Just keep reflecting their feelings back to them."

"Sometimes during conflict, because they align with feelings and you align by thoughts, their conception of your behavior is that you are insane. There is no path for them to mentally assimilate how you are engaging and disengaging in the conflict, so they deduce you are crazy."

"It is very hard to explain to some people how they have an effect in the world. If you are trying to help them they <u>hear,</u> 'I am bad and/or I have to change.' Let's say that I am swimming in the ocean with my young sons. They climb on my head, pushing me under and I can't breathe. They are having an effect—I can't breathe, I could drown. If I fuss at them they *hear* me saying, 'You're trying to kill me and you are bad.' I am just explaining the effect they're having not judging whether they are good or bad."

"If someone is asking/demanding something of you and they are being a mature adult then they ask equally willing to take the pain of receiving a 'no.' It is not a free request, or mature unless they will love and treat you the same with or after a 'no.' If they do not or will not treat you the same if you give a 'no', they are asking as a child asks. Children get very upset when told 'no.'

ON RELATING WITH WOUNDED PEOPLE

Since I was living with and trying to minister to my new housemates, many of my conversations with JW were about questions I had about helping others who were deeply wounded. Although we were working on my issues, he continued to be my mentor as well as helping me with my own pain. These are some of the jewels he gave me about relating with wounded people, and/or those adults stuck at the infant and child stage of maturity. These were given to me, and practiced by me, over many months and were a large part of my new identity and ways of relating.

"The wounded person can only deal with their pain to the level that they have joy in their life. Building joy is the goal, not recovery."

"We can help wounded people by having enough joy to sit with them in their pain and help them learn to return to joy."

"If a person did not learn to return to joy from a certain emotion, they will make strategies to keep from feeling the ones they did not learn that path back to joy from."

(For an in-depth discussion about joy, please look at those chapters in *The Life Model*.)

"When bonded with wounded people, sometimes we get more pain in a week than most people get in their lifetime, both from hearing their stories and from their dysfunction."

"Coming and going will look like abandonment to a wounded person."

"A wounded person may reject you in order to watch how you handle rejection and survive. It gives them hope that they can make it. We must be willing to stand at the foot of the cross where

He shows up. They want to see many things they have not seen as a child. It takes them in deeply, to discover who they were made to be. Their hearts tell them there is hope that things can be real. They hear us say it is real and then they test us to see if it is real. What a tremendous joy for us to see who they really are and watch pure life coming right out of them and touching others."

"When someone you are helping gets angry at you, remember that they have a difficult time telling the difference between past and present pain."

"Whenever you are in your 'messed-up-ness, God will put you with someone who needs your messed-up-ness."

"Listen for themes and tones in what people are saying, not just content."

"I have spent weeks to find the best way to say something and it will still cause a blow-up. Some truth just hurts no matter how we say it."

"It is one thing to help a weak person and another to sponsor bad habits."

"When you see a problem with someone that looks like it will not turn out well, it is an important reason for you to be very upset. You see things that you know will not work and will be very painful for them in the long run. But if they will not listen to your wisdom, you will have to bear the pain of knowing and watching."

"I confront very low key without the expectation that a change or even understanding will result."

"Don't mix up love and trust. You can still love someone you don't trust."

"Remember this when a wounded one cannot keep their promises: It is like when a little child says, 'I will stay awake and wait for you, Mommy.' Peter promised he would die and meant it. But he did not yet have a solid enough self to stay with what he really wanted."

"Wounded people will hear your tone and watch your face more than your words. If you are not getting *some* eye contact then you are wasting your time. They were not delighted in as a baby, but got hurt over and over. Much of what you communicate is non verbal."

"You feel badly when you upset someone. Everyone is an upsetting person. You are trying not to be one, instead of accepting that you are a real upsetting person. Jesus was a very upsetting person—he upset lots of folks. He doesn't want to be with people who do all things right, but with people who are willing to admit they are upsetting. You lack peace about being an upsetting person.

Given that you are an upsetting person, how will you express that as you? ('Not with yelling', I said) Sort out the best way to express that you are an all around upsetting person. When you are with a person with major hurts you will upset them even more. It may not show up until later. Don't stop loving or disconnect the bond when they are upset."

"The difference in a healthy system of relating and an unhealthy one is the difference in linear and circular causality (or thinking). Circular is more healthy. For example—I did this to you-that caused this- that contributed to this. No one then can establish blame because it is impossible to be completely innocent. The causes go both ways. It is the only way out of an abusive situation. For example if my 'adopted daughter' screams at me, it will cause an effect. I will pull back and heal. She will learn how her behavior has an effect of 'losing me' for a season. On the other hand, linear thinking says, 'I did this, and it made you do this--so you abused me.' This way blame is established but the relationship is hurt. Our culture says it has to be someone's fault and many have to prove it is someone else's."

Speaking further about finding fault, JW again reminded me of the sarx or as he sometimes calls it "picker."

"A Biblically informed picker is the worst kind. It tries to determine who is at fault by picking the right thing to do or that should have been done. It kills inside if we try to pick the right thing when the heart does not line up. When we ignore our picker, we follow our Father. God never asks, 'Who is at fault here? He only asks, 'What happened here?' We are just witnesses."

Many times after conflict in my new household, I would not be spoken to for days. It hurt very much, but I struggled that it was my fault for speaking to issues at all. JW had a jewel for these feelings:

"In a conflict, when we feel powerless, we take that something is our fault, thinking then that we can change it. Then when we reach the point where we can't negotiate with the other person, we want to settle ourselves inside and adjust ourselves so that it won't hurt so much. It does hurt and will always hurt when someone quits listening to you.

It is just like you to feel this hurt. Is there something wrong with you? Well, God is upset when we disengage from Him and don't listen. It hurts Him. So you are like Him. The upside of this for you is that the meek shall inherit the earth. You are in an in-depth course in meekness, humility, softness. Your character will benefit from this as you remember that it is supposed to hurt and keep loving in spite of the hurt."

When I lost it emotionally with my new household, I felt terrible and had many self-depreciating thoughts. I hated myself when I hurt anyone, especially if I did not mean to. I always liked JW's illustrations.

"This is the ideal—suppose you had a baby and dropped him and banged his head. Your immediate response is to move close and comfort. This is the normal way. At some age, most people learn to get angry and push away from the one that hurt them. If you really hurt them and they won't let you close, then you hate yourself. This is a response to powerlessness—self-hatred. You can make bad things happen but not good things. As long as you believe inside that bad things are all you can make happen, you will hate yourself. First you feel frustration at doing a bad thing, then you try to get close, and if the other gets more upset, it gets worse and worse down to self- hatred. This is such a horrible view of our humanity. The popular belief about Romans 7 is 'I can only do bad things.' If you do bad things to yourself, (beat up on yourself), the person who is doing bad things, at least they are done to the right person. If we consider ourselves to be bad after causing someone pain, then if we cause pain we are automatically bad and we stand condemned. Causing pain is not always bad.

"In relating with wounded people we cause pain and they don't like it. Then God has to heal. Everyone tells us from childhood up that we are bad if we hurt someone. When mature, we want to suffer with them when causing pain. If they let us get close, then we can suffer with them, and that is ok, but if they push away, it is very hard and painful. We feel powerless. Since closeness increases the pain, they interpret it that we are bad for hurting them. Then the best part of you is called bad, the part that wants to love, soothe, be with.

You hurt from not being able to come close after the hurt. The antidote for you is, 'I am really a good person.' On a practical level, take an active approach: 'One of the things I like about me is that I am able to cause pain even when they don't understand.' It takes a while to grow maturity to say this. But I know you will stay engaged even when you wish you could stop."

This was thought-provoking, so I asked JW for clarification: 'What is the difference in me accepting or liking the part of me that can hurt someone and the people who have hurt me so much that I have to stay away from them?"

"The people who hurt you made no attempt to either acknowledge, accept or get to like the part of them that could hurt you, so they never found out what God's intended purpose would be. We can only find out His purpose when we admit and accept that part. We do that with 'bad' alters (other personalities within a person with Dissociative Identity Disorder.) all the time."

"If we are truly harming a person it is important to protect them from ourselves. Try to explain that you have to be apart if that is happening. A wounded person has never watched an abuser say, 'I might have to protect you from me.'"

"You can't do much of anything to get something to turn out right if the other person holds the standard for what 'turn out right' will look like."

Another jewel JW gave me was to help me keep from losing my cool when in a heated discussion with a wounded person. He said, "If you cannot be 'invisible'—leave immediately." This meant that in a heated discussion or problem, if I were not able to focus on the other and leave my part out of it, I should leave and calm myself, then try the discussion later.

After a particularly trying time when someone I loved was going out with a person that didn't seem very quality, I was feeling very upset. JW explained why it hurt me so much to watch.

"When we are in a life-sharing bond with someone who is under the adult stage or unable to take care of themselves, other bonds they make will take us into that bond with them. For example, when our child is bonded with someone that we know and love, it is a great thing—for them to have this other loving bond. But when they connect with someone we have no bond with it can feel horrible. They take us into the same things they are doing with that other person and it is unbearable. In First Corinthians we see how Jesus is bonded with a prostitute. He is forced into the same activity, dragged into something that is not of His nature."

This conversation brought me a deeper inner knowing of my oneness with Jesus and in His sufferings. I asked Him, crying out, 'How do you bear loving all these people who never bid you the time of day, completely ignore you and never see you as you really are? Only God could bear that number! How do you bear being bonded and taken to horrible places? I do not want to take you anywhere out of your nature. You truly are wearing my body. You are in everything.' (1 Corinthians 6: 2-20, Colossians 1:24, Philippians 3:8)

ON SAYING "OUCH"

I had to learn not to get so upset when my expressed wishes or needs were turned into blame and accusations towards my heart. That was part of learning to live peacefully with my housemates and act like myself in all situations. With his usual wit and catchy ways of describing things, JW called this learning to say "Ouch." I was used to being able to say ouch with some people, but my housemates often got very upset with my ouches. These jewels were very insightful for me.

"An 'ouch' is just an 'ouch' in a family that is running right. It is nothing—it just helps us get the comfort we need, even if it is from ourselves. (There are many ways to get comfort.)

"It is not bad to have an ouch. It just means you need comfort."

"If you don't acknowledge the ouch you can't even comfort yourself."

"If you back down from ouches the others involved won't learn."

" Here is an example on saying ouch from one of my friends: My friend had a three year old daughter in a day care. She got poked all the time by other kids, but didn't say anything. But at home, she poked her daddy in the eye and he said, 'ouch'. He always said ouch and she realized that the kids had hurt her, too. When someone hurts you, you have to say, 'ouch.' Every time. We don't let even a baby poke us in the eye without saying, 'ouch.'"

One whole letter was addressed to saying ouch:

"First, 'Ouches' are usually *sark* (flesh) infested (Remember JW's definition: we are plagued by the impression that we can tell good from evil on our own. * P. 238 *R. D.*). For hurt people, ouches usually carry messages about who is bad or who is good, who is messed up (lacks value) and who has worth. There is often a *sark* rule in their thinking that says 'people with more value can say, 'You hurt me,' to people of less value'. Watch very carefully any discussion that comes after an 'ouch.' The *sark* will attack you either inside at yourself or make you defensive."

"Second, beware of any discussion of household rules after an ouch. Ouches are not about rules-- they are about people. If you must discuss a rule, do it later—like the next day. Violating rules do not make ouches. 'Man was not made for the Sabbath.'

"Third, ouches are not MOSTLY about change. If you start discussing change after an ouch, you missed the point. Ouches are about the things that don't change—your hearts. You always want to comfort an ouch for someone you see hurting—even an enemy. Don't discuss what should change until first everyone is comforted."

"Finally, when you say ouch to someone, be fairly certain that their empathy will give them a resonant ouch and their *sark* will kick their heads. One ouch will lead to two being comforted every time. You will need to teach this to everyone."

"If a lawn mower goes over your foot or the begonias, you say, 'Ouch!' and tell the person mowing that you will show them a better way. Shrugging it off does not teach them what you want them to learn."

"It hurts you deeply when someone denies that something ever happened that has hurt you. You are not allowed to say 'ouch' and cannot discuss and solve the problem."

"When you are feeling irritated by not being listened to, check to see if you have said ouch. Go through your journal and see how many times you have suppressed an ouch. Part of the irritation can be from the past, but much here is from a build up of all the things you can't say ouch about. Some do not know how to say ouch or hear an ouch and say, 'I'm sorry.' Make it part of normal living to say ouch. It is like me to say ouch. If someone steps on my foot, I say ouch, but I do not have to teach them to walk. In a family that is running right, an ouch is an ouch. When there is lots of dysfunction, you probably wont get the response back that you want; you will probably get cannon balls.

You get in trouble a lot when you say ouch, but it is something you cannot suppress because it is like you to say ouch. If you back down no one will learn that an ouch is just an ouch. How do you know when to say ouch? Simple-- does it or does it not hurt, destabilize you, make you feel yucky inside? For better or worse it is just an ouch. The reason is so you can get comfort, even from yourself. When others learn to say ouch they will love the comfort. Ouches just mean you need comfort."

ON ALLOWING HARM

My jewels from JW about allowing someone to hurt me were a little different from the ones about saying "ouch." These kinds of hurts would be more along the lines of loud verbal attacks, hateful, untrue accusations or some kind of harmful intent. Examples of this might be hurtful sarcasm, hurtful joking, public put downs, or ugly gossip. I had been in the habit for years of trying to ignore hurts by not responding to them, and afterwards taking them to Jesus. JW was helping me break free from this unhealthy response.

"Do not allow harm. If you think it is coming you can say something like, 'Do you intend to hurt me right now? If so I will stop you and we will find a better way'."

"If you allow someone to hurt a valuable and precious you, you are hurting them."

I had never looked at allowing hurt as not being good for the other person. It made sense though, because the other person would never have to face their own issues about why they were hurting someone. Agape love would want the best for that other, not enable their wrong behavior. I also remembered that one of the adult level tasks is to protect others from oneself if one is not okay.

Like JW's jewel about picking up my car, this jewel was very significant. Again he used the physical world to make an emotional point.

"You do not, never have and never shall handle shooting (verbally abusive attacks) well. End the discussion when the gun is pulled out. It is OK to take steps to keep from being shot. If you try to explain, it means you think you can handle being shot. Gunshot pain is not manageable. If you are hemorrhaging and losing blood, no one asks you to do your best algebra. You have to get to a first aid station and emergency protocol goes into effect. You may have to go away to recover and get your blood count back up."

"If someone says they are trying to help you, check to see if they are putting gasoline in your blood transfusion. No contaminated blood—you cannot have even 1% gasoline—it must be 100% clear!"

Condemnation, untimely advise, Spiritual abuse, trying to fix instead of listening or comforting, adding pain to the pain are examples of gasoline in a blood transfusion. Those types of help are toxic, contaminated help, not help at all and to be quickly avoided when noticed.

ON HAVING NO COMMUNITY SUPPORT

While I was living with my adopted family and later they with me, many in my community did not understand and they were against what I felt God had told me to do. Lack of community support (church) was addressed often with JW. Like so much of my pain, he certainly knew from experience about having little to no support. I felt almost hopeless again over some more rejections from church leaders, especially when I felt that I was doing a God-like thing. JW continued to tell me who I am:

"You are wonderful and I like you the way you are. You are kind and loving with a good heart. You have my respect. Be glad and respect yourself. You are dealing with some rigid people and rigid people tend to snap and break instead of bend and accommodate. You are good to sacrifice for them to be able to process some feelings, but let them know when you give a boundary and they do not listen. Pray that some of them will bend."

"People will not understand the kind of home you want to make. You will feel you have crawled out of water onto a hostile beach because the world you live in is so different. When they do not understand, it has undertones of 'why are you doing this crazy thing you are doing?'"

I really found that to be true when I tried to share with my pastor about caring for and helping deeply wounded people. I came away from that meeting feeling like my treasures had been stomped on. He thought I was into something not Biblical and that Biblical principles are all that is needed to change people. I felt very sad in my different world and I knew from experience that he was wrong.

"Church leaders like to keep things under control and not be overwhelmed. There is a time to be overwhelmed. Some people shrink their world in order to not feel overwhelmed. It would be better to voluntarily allow themselves to be overwhelmed."

One day God gave me a respite while holding my newest granddaughter, Elysia, a precious newborn. It felt so good to hold her and just enjoy looking at her. She couldn't perform in any way except with smiles and she didn't do anything except be herself. She was delightful to behold and I experienced great joy just being with her. Jesus whispered softly in my heart, "This is how you are to Me. I enjoy and delight in being with you; in you just being yourself." My heart was touched deeply because I could see what He meant. JW agreed and pointed out:

"When we deeply love someone (like I did Margaret and her children), we need others to joy and delight in them, not see them as a pain or bad. If they are not enjoyed, the parent part of us gets very injured and the injury is excruciating and hard to describe."

JW was right. It was very hurtful when those around me did not understand that I had my adopted family with me because God said to. It was not easy, but it was what He told me to do.

"You are attacked more for being kind than being mean. More for being truthful, generous, and loving than ever for lying, etc. The ones who are saying you are bad are attacking your heart, telling you the 'right thing to do.'"

"When you meet people you expect them to be like you: friendly, kind, open, truthful. You are shocked when they are mean."

"When someone says you are stingy and greedy, you can thank them for reminding you how truly generous you are."

After months of anger and conflict that came from several directions, God touched me afresh while I was at church in a youth prayer meeting led by my oldest son, Jim. I literally felt God's presence upon me and heard in my heart again, "You are right on time." I did not realize I was feeling so badly for not releasing some of my problems and "getting back to normal" more quickly. God also reassured me that I had been obedient in the face of much flak. I realized how deeply alone I'd been and felt like I had stepped out of the darkest, longest tunnel imaginable. I was on my face before God, knowing I was called to a very difficult task and that I was to stand in the face of opposition until He released me.

As time passed, I began to settle into my new circumstances. The other teen moved on as did Margaret's own. They came and went over the years. Margaret was making progress also in her recovery. JW told me during one conversation after I told him of a secular book I had read that helped me understand Margaret better—"It just delights me to hear what you have done with some of the books you have read. One of them is quite dead-set against my philosophy and you have a big enough self to read it, take in what is good and use it. I would love to have you show a flock of therapists that can't do what you have done." This was a great and kind compensation for much of the pain I had experienced from misunderstanding people. I felt joy that Margaret was progressing and that we were relating better again.

ON 'THE WIFE'

In October of 1998, I was still grieving quite a bit of the time. At church that week, I was deeply touched by God and by a song my daughter-in-law, Elizabeth, sang. Also that day when the pastor was teaching, my son, Greg, leaned over and said, "What he is saying is you, Mom." It was a very loving complement, though I cannot remember the details except that it had something to do with servant hood and being like Jesus. This encounter with God through my son and church service caused many tears and JW had a lot of work to do the next two or three phone calls.

JW helped me begin exploring that there was another part of me split apart from BOJ that was not about the rape issues or "bad girl." We called her 'the wife." Just before this phone call, I had had a dream. The dream seemed to be related to the wife. In the dream, I had cut off my hands and feet. I had no idea what this meant.

After sharing the dream with JW he gave me questions to ponder: "There is the Barbara (BOJ) that I know. She is the loving, nurturing bonding you. 'The wife' is sad, not enjoyed, needs validation from others, loves to help but not appreciated, the counselor, still rejects herself, the crushed one. 'The wife' pushed BOJ away because she got in trouble when BOJ came around. Not everyone is that bothered by being in trouble. Why is it so big? What do you have to believe differently here in order to be healed? What has to change? Why did 'the wife' want to kill her hands in the dream? What would you <u>not</u> have if you stopped being the wife?" I had to think about these questions. I didn't immediately know the answers.

The next weekend I went to a retreat for my teaching job at a Christian school. During one of the sessions I was almost overcome by grief over something the speaker said and I could hardly maintain my composure. I was there in a room full of loving, caring people but I had to struggle to keep from bursting into tears. The pain was too big and would have scared people, but I know the struggle to maintain composure showed on my face. As soon as the session ended, I rushed to my car to release very, very deep pain. I sat there sobbing loudly. It was deep grieving about my failed marriage, along with processing some unpleasant things that had transpired with my job. The next time I was with the group, no one asked me if I was all right. This fed my painful history of not being comforted by my Christian community. I felt very alone. (A wise friend later told me "This is a good example of "how" to hurt, accept and validate one's own pain all at the same time.")

During the next phone call JW explored some more about 'the wife'. It seemed her issue had something to do with wanting to help others and not being affirmed for it. She needed and wanted validation and approval from other Christians--husband, family, community.

"'The wife' tried to help in various ways through the years but was crushed and possibly became so hopeless that she vowed not to try anymore. Feeling crushed comes from not being listened to and becoming disconnected; from not being regarded, from being told that your feelings don't matter, and from things you are interested in not being shared in joy."

These words were touching me deeply and crushed was a good description of how I felt.

JW asked me what crushed looks like, but before I could answer, he answered his own question. "We normally expect whatever is crushed to not function anymore. Something that is broken can be fixed, but something that is crushed can't be put back together." (I told Jesus I did not ever want to do this to anyone.)

He then went back to 'the wife.' I think you unknowingly lamented, 'No one sees me as a good Christian,' until that Sunday when Greg affirmed that part of you. Now the wife is one of those bad Christians that gets a divorce. The young Bringer of Joy part settled for being misunderstood by other Christians. 'The wife's' pain is a little different. It comes from her lack of recognition and affirmation."

It was very hard for me to look at this and understand it because it sounded prideful and wrong to want to be affirmed.

"This is <u>not</u> a bad thing to want," JW assured me. It is another legitimate need that was not met, and you were crushed when you got little affirmation and appreciation for trying to help. You did not quit trying for a very long time; you tried even when you were hopeless that those needs would be met. You finally gave up inside. Let me ask you this--Are you glad when your adopted daughter, Margaret, or any of your children, gets admired and appreciated? 'Oh, yes,' I answered. 'I love it and it happens all the time.'

JW said very softly, 'You need it as much as she does. 'The wife' part of you believes it is bad to want recognition because of teachings on pride. You may have thrown the baby out with the bath water. BOJ knows it is not true, but she had already settled for being misunderstood by Christians when her friends turned away. All along you've needed affirmation and hardly got any. If there is <u>any</u> legitimate need that is not recognized, couldn't that be damaging to a person? Remember that neglect or lack is a trauma.

You are a daughter of the King who can't come out and dance because you gave up inside and you still fear the rejection you got when you needed affirmation and comfort. You like to dance; you want to dance. Why wouldn't they see it? They saw you as a bad person.

They rejected you for <u>*good*</u> things. Can you believe you were even rejected for being honest? You just wanted someone to say, 'See her, the wonderful helpmeet, the wonderful Christian, the nurturer, the good student, the good analyzer, the good mommy, the honest and moral one."

JW asked Jesus to take me back to the root beginning of this. Jesus showed me the root began when my husband and I joined the staff of Campus Crusade and the pattern had continued ever since. I could remember several times through the years when I'd asked for help, especially concerning Jim's anger, and instead of love and affirmation I very often got blame and rejection, both from Jim and the people who were supposed to help us grow and learn. I believed what my leaders and friends told me through the years—that I was bad and to blame.

JW continued that conversation: "There is no part of ourselves we can see, good or bad about ourselves, without another person. You needed something for years and were not getting it. Nothing you did or said helped. Why? That is Satan's standard warfare. He does not want us to get what we need because it will directly help us--and the Body of Christ. You couldn't get it from churches, Christian schools, peers—anywhere--or you would soar and dance. When the power of this stronghold is broken, the Rivers will flow again."

By now during this call, I had cried buckets full of tears. I said through the tears, "It really hurt when I was not affirmed and got stones when I asked for bread, but it hurt even more to be put down for being myself."

As we continued to talk, I could see that under the hurt was also a lot of anger because I had asked for help, even begged for it and received blame instead. JW told me that after I hung up the phone I needed to scream out the anger at not being helped. I knew several ways to get my anger out. Sometimes I went to the woods beside my house and picked up a large stick from the ground and hit it against a tree until it shattered into a thousand pieces. I might break several limbs and sticks. Sometimes I threw ice off the deck into the yard. Sometimes when I was alone, I literally screamed and screamed.

Before hanging up the phone, I quietly asked JW, 'Am I bad?' He answered very softly, *"Jesus, is she bad?"* I started to cry again. 'Am I bad for leaving?' He said again, *"Jesus is she bad?"* I cried some more. He said, *"The screams are stifled because you need support from your church community and Christians, and do not have it. These kinds of feelings are very difficult to process without support."*

My other homework for the evening after the phone conversation was to take each memory I had of being told things were my fault and take them to Jesus one by one and ask Him for the truth of each one. I took some time to do that. Jesus assured me they were not all my fault.

There was another issue that 'the wife' struggled with. She felt a loss of value whenever she caused someone pain. JW said that he had struggled with the same thing.

"We can hurt someone with the truth or even a need we have. If one walks in the truth, one will hurt people. You have been taking that your value diminishes when you cause pain. You need someone to come along side and say, 'She still has value even if she does make bad choices or hurt someone.' The wife had a double whammy wound—she was blamed, devalued and neglected. Then not only did the Christian community not stand up and say, 'She is valuable,' they reinforced the problem by communicating to her that she was bad."

"The pain you have carried from your lack of support from your community was like a farmer trying to plow without a plow. People asked him why didn't he farm all his land? He thinks he is not a good farmer. He just had a hand tool, a spade. If he'd had a plow he could have done better. He always thought something was wrong with *him* for not having a plow. Do we look at an abused person and say, 'What's wrong with you for needing a family? Why didn't you just grow up right anyway?' There's something important about the family of God on Earth, isn't there? We take it that we should have made it work anyway, without support from God's family."

These jewels were helping me find the answers to the questions that JW had asked during the first conversation about the wife issue: "Why was I so bothered by getting in trouble? What had to change for me to be healed and what would I not have if I quit being 'the wife?' Why did I cut off my hands in my dream?"

Getting in trouble, as I called it, had long been a hurtful problem for me because almost every time I went to someone for help with my 'wife' pain, I was told it was all me and if I would only do this or that, everything would be okay. It also hurt very much to get in trouble with my community and husband at times when I was just being myself. For example when I was honest or spoke the truth, it was often communicated to me that somehow I was bad. Analyzing irritated Jim. Holding people accountable made some uncomfortable. I began to better understand that when I was truthful with people, and they got upset, that I was not bad or wrong to say the truth in love. And I was careful to say it in love.

JW's jewels helped with the other questions as well. In order to be healed, I would have to know that all conflicts or problems were not my fault and see that I was not bad for needing affirmation and support. I was hurting from a legitimate need. Just the weekly comfort and understanding I received from JW had already helped me be able to even look at these issues and try to process them.

I realized that cutting off my hands in my dream was a symbol for the pain I felt when my desire to help people continually brought misinterpretations of my heart. Inside I was crying, "Get rid of those helping hands that only bring misunderstanding and pain." Having my heart misinterpreted was very painful. It would be easier to quit helping.

If this part of me called 'the wife' had healing, then what would I not have any longer? I would not have the unhealthy permission I gave others to tell me who I am. I would not have my identity so tied up in a role. Also I would not have limitations on my dancing and soaring with God. I would have freedom!

ON FOLLOWING MY HEART

Recently I had made a life-changing decision about my job at the Christian school where I had been teaching. I often doubted myself, and my ability to hear God about that decision, because the result did not look good. Then I made another decision that looked like a big mistake. (I can hear the sark now as I write) JW told me,

"You do not give yourself the kind of freedom for making decisions that you give Margaret. You made a life changing decision that turned out crappy and then settled in to bear it the rest of your life. Now you are beating up on yourself for another one. There are more than one or two choices in the world. American Christianity elevates the will to an enormous place. It says, 'Come hell or high water we will follow this out....' This is the *sark* again. 'I have to figure out the right thing to do. Decisions are irreversible.'

The better question than 'Did I make the right choice?' is "Do we want condemnation for choices we make or will we look at effects we are having on others?' It is much more important to learn about the effects we have on the world around us, than it is to believe we have to go down with the ship over decisions. You need grace from the Christian community and when you do not get it, grieve and follow your heart. You may have to ride with a skunk, (*consequences*) but you do not have to brush its fur (*make things worse by beating up on yourself*)."

Next JW reminded me about the bent arrows:

"When I am doing archery, my bent arrows never go the way I aim. People are crooked arrows and can't go straight. We are too bent to hit the target, so give up and let the Archer hit it. Ask God whenever you think you made a wrong decision after praying about it, 'What were you shooting at God, when I made that decision?'"

It was such a relief to take these words and apply them, to rest in God's love. It wasn't long until I saw that God was definitely in my decision about school, even though right afterwards it looked like a wrong one. The next school year, 1999-2000, I had a very good experience teaching at a public school.

In June 2000, I made another life-changing decision. Exhausted with teaching school and unable to resolve the recurring conflict with my adopted family, I sold my house and moved in with my third son, Greg, and Chris and their family. At last I could truly rest and finish processing all the changes that had come to me. What a joy to watch Greg with his little daughter—making her a sandwich, playing with her, bathing her. What a joy to see him go to the store with his wife when he had planned to go outside and 'work.' How great it felt to have them both come and tell me, "I'm glad you are here." I could hardly get over such wonder that Chris would have me there and was my friend. I missed my adopted family deeply, but I knew in my heart that things were not going to work out with living together. It was time to rest and go on. It was a great new beginning for a tired and lonely Bringer of Joy. But the healing did not end.

ON BEING MISJUDGED

In October 2000, God touched another aspect of my wounds. I went to Texas to be with my sister and her husband, to attend a seminar that they sponsored. During the first weekend, this seminar resurrected every feeling I ever had or thought about my Christian community's lack of affirmation, understanding and support. It was horrible. When I returned home, JW walked me through the pain and helped me see that as in the past, at this seminar, again people were judging me without really knowing me inside.

"The stuff from the seminar landed right on that past pain of being misjudged. Most seminars are set up to blast denial and you are not in denial. They cannot evaluate you without knowing you. Because you have had much pain from your community group, you desperately need a group to recognize your pain. You need a group to say, "'I'm sorry.' You need a group to see and admit what they did to you and ask your forgiveness, to see your pain and not mistake it for defensiveness or worry. You need them to admit they treated you unfairly and that what they were saying did not fit you, but rather injured you further. You need hope from a group, instead of accusations that you're in denial. The seminar leaders were running you through a program instead of seeing you. Because you always have an open spirit to hear what's wrong with you, you are so easily stomped on. This landed on the message that's been given to you, 'It is not okay to be okay. There is something about you that is bad that you don't know about.'"

I had to cling to these jewels. It was still difficult for me to believe that those in "authority" might be wrong. I thanked God for JW and how he saw me and knew me so that I could hear the truth. And God went a step further when I went back the next weekend to finish the seminar. God brought to pass exactly what JW said I needed. During one of the exercises, where again the leader of my small group was trying to blast my denial when I said I was okay, one of the women in my small group stood up to the leader and said, 'You are doing to her the very thing she is trying to tell you has happened to her in the past.' She then hugged me and I began to weep. The leader said to me softly, as he had been trained, 'Just let it go, let it go.' The lady said to him, "BE QUIET!" My dam of tears burst! That was exactly what I needed the most. I needed someone to understand and then stand up for me.

Later I told another one of the leaders of the seminar, "If you saw a person lying on the sidewalk cut in half, would you say, 'Just let it go'?" "No! You would say, as Jesus would, 'Come, my Child, and be healed. You need to be in a comfort zone not out of it'." All of us involved at the seminar worked it through with love and caring, and I have never been quite the same since that seminar. It was a life-changing experience in several ways, and I would highly recommend it! God knew what I needed.

JW told me that my capacity to explain and protect myself was being revived as I walked through these different experiences. We realized that I had an inner vow that needed breaking here concerning authorities. Somewhere along the way, I had declared to myself, "I will not keep telling an authority who I am if they won't listen." In prayer we broke this vow. I could now return to joy from the despair of so many not listening to me or wanting to be with me. In the future it would be a lot easier to discern when someone who did not know my heart tried to tell me who I am. JW reminded me:

"Persist in two things—being yourself as much as possible. If there is a problem, let it be known you want a response from others so you can work it out and return to joy with them."

ON JOY

I continue to have contact with JW and learn from him. Joy and how the brain works are the current topics. He is writing more books and the latest called *Living With Men* contains great detail about joy and how God made our brains and our lives to be filled with joy, beginning in infancy. I see in JW's lessons about joy, the greatness of God in a new way and how so many Scripture verses fit into the physical part of us. It makes me think of how God told the Israelites about food and hygiene when they, nor anyone else, knew about germs. Now people are studying the brain and how joy and bonding are so vital to the human experience, and we Christians can put it all together with the Scripture, just as more modern men actually saw the germs and understood Deuteronomy better as technology progressed.

I say this about joy to encourage you to study the many verses in the Bible about joy, *The Life Model, Living With Men* and other writings about joy, because God and JW say it better than I could. It would take another book to say all that I have learned about this and how it has especially changed my views of relating to people and about child rearing. I sprinkled some of it here and there within the jewels. JW's constant insistence that I was/am Bringer of Joy changed my life. He told me only who I am through the heart that Jesus gave me and Heaven's eyes. That is how I try to live my life now, both with myself and with others in my life, truly being a Bringer of Joy.

THE PRESENT

Many years have passed since the intense years I spent receiving jewels from God through JW. JW was the earthly vessel that God used to help me. I thank God for that, because without him I don't think I would be here. How wonderful it is now that I struggle less and live in joy more. My life is contented and full of love from family and close friends. I don't know what the future holds for me, but I do know that God is totally faithful. It's great now, when the Lord does allow, to share the jewels from my treasure chest by which God so richly blessed me through JW. I pray that your life will also be enriched, by poring over JW's Jewels. Savor them slowly and often that you, too, might grow and flourish as the Lord's jewel. May 2006.

The following is a list of *some* of the books that I read that contain information about union or the Exchanged Life. For a complete list of books that you can purchase on the Exchanged Life, go to www.crosslifebooks.com or www.elmcolo.org. Much of what I learned was in person or through cassette tapes.

The Rest of the Gospel	Dan Stone
Handbook to Happiness	Dr. Charles Solomon
The Ins and Out of Rejection	Dr. Charles Solomon
Birthright	David Needham
Lifetime Guarantee	Dr. Bill Gillham
The Confident Woman	Anabel Gillham
Absolute Surrender	Andrew Murray
Turkeys and Eagles	Peter Lord
Hinds Feet on High Places	Hannah Hurnard
Rees Howells Intercessor	Norman Grubb
The Key to Everything	Norman Grubb
Man Alive	John Whittle
Cry of the Human Heart	Juan Carlos Ortiz
The Normal Christian Life	Watchman Nee
Table in the Wilderness	Watchman Nee

Hudson Taylor's Spiritual Secret	Dr. and Mrs. Howard Taylor
Living the Spirit Filled Life	Dr. Bill Bright
Families Where Grace is In Place	Jeff VanVonderen
Defeating Dark Angels	Dr. Charles Kraft
Deep Wounds, Deep Healing	Dr. Charles Kraft

And of course *The Red Dragon Cast Down* Dr. E. James Wilder

Unless noted, all Bible references are from the New American Standard Version for clarification of the words "flesh" and "old self" or "sin nature," as some versions make it difficult to note that the two words are not the same in the Greek.

Made in the USA
Columbia, SC
24 March 2021